THE MAKING OF THE BIBLE

The Making of the Bible

WILLIAM BARCLAY

THE SAINT ANDREW PRESS
EDINBURGH

First published in 1961 by
THE LUTTERWORTH PRESS, London.
Reprinted in 1961.

Published in 1979
and updated in 1991 by
THE SAINT ANDREW PRESS
121 George Street, Edinburgh EH2 4YN.

ISBN 0 7152 0420 3

Most of the quotations in this book are from the REVISED
STANDARD VERSION (RSV), copyright 1946, 1952, © 1971,
by the Division of Christian Education of the National Council of
the Churches of Christ in the USA, and are used by permission.

Quotations from the Authorized or King James Version are denoted as AV.

ISBN-0-7152-0420-3

This book has been set in 11/12.5 pt Times Roman.

Printed and Bound by Bell and Bain Ltd., Glasgow

Contents

Preface

by Ronald Barclay

'IF YOU WANT to keep alive, keep learning'. That was one of my father's favourite statements and this book is a reflection of his belief that learning more about the Bible and its history is an important part of our lives. He used to tell people how bitterly disappointed he felt when he discovered in second-hand bookshops some of the texts he had been lecturing on in Divinity College to his students. He could not understand how anyone could sell the tools of the trade, and his view never changed throughout his life —that 'to think is a necessity of the Christian life'.

Of course, he knew that thinking and reading and learning is only one facet of the Christian life, and he recognized in all of his books the part played by out hearts, by our faith and by the Holy Spirit in our deeper understanding of God's word.

My father used to claim that he was not a great scholar and that he never had an original thought in his life! Personally, I think that he was too hard on himself. He used to call himself a 'theological middleman', and this book is a good example of his claim that his expertise lay in collecting ideas together, and collating them, so that everyone, scholar and non-scholar alike, 'the ordinary man and his wife', as he put it, could understand immediately the material and ideas being presented. He loved to appeal to the unchurched masses to learn more about the Bible and Jesus, and to make decisions for themselves, based on the material he was presenting.

In this book he collects and collates with great skill all

the information necessary for us to understand how the Bible we use today came into being. From his early ministry in Trinity Church, Renfrew, onwards, he always placed great emphasis on understanding not just the origins, but also the context of the Bible, especially the background to the life and teachings of Jesus. He believed that it helped us to come closer to the words of the Bible, particularly to Jesus' words, if we understood the life and times of the those people who fill the pages of the Bible. One critic said, in a rather unkind manner, 'That man Barclay, he's the one who can tell you what Jesus had for breakfast!' My father would probably have taken that as a compliment.

This book helps us to understand the history of the making of the Bible and thus fulfills my father's long-held aim to give practical and relevant assistance to everyone who wants to know more about God's word. My hope for you, the reader, is that, in my father's words, 'the more you know about the Bible, the greater the Bible becomes'.

February 1991

Foreword

(adapted from the original publication)

IN ANY UNDERTAKING of study the first essential is to define the area of study. This is precisely what I hope will be achieved in this book. In it I seek to define the Bible, and to explore how it came to be in the form in which it exists today.

To give it its technical name, this book seeks to deal with the *Canon* of Holy Scripture, and to tell the story of the formation of the Canon. For some reason or another the study of the Canon of Holy Scripture has come to be looked upon as one of the dry and less interesting fields of Bible study. That is a great pity, for it is by the study of the formation of the Canon that we come to see the essential greatness of Scripture.

As we study the history of the Bible, and as we come to see how it came to be what it is today, we see God speaking to men and women in every age and generation through those whom his Spirit inspired, and through events by which he made his Will known to all people. We see that word of God establishing itself in the hearts and minds of mankind. We see the necessities of the human situation driving men to seek and to study and to cling to the word of God. We see the events of history and the needs of the human heart sending people for strength and guidance, for help and for comfort to the word of God.

Above all we come to see how the Bible came to be the Bible, how these books came to be regarded as Holy Scripture; how they came to be regarded not simply as great books, but as *holy* books; not simply as the products of the mind and pen of great men, but as products of the divine inspiration of the Spirit of God. We come to see quite clearly when we study the formation of the Canon of Scripture, that the Bible and the books of the Bible came to be regarded as the inspired word of God, not because of any decision of any Synod or Council or Committee or Church, but because in them mankind found God.

The supremely important thing is not what men did to these books, but what these books did to men.

These books, as the story plainly shows, became Scripture because nothing could stop them doing so. Their unique inspiration was self-evidencing through their ability to meet the needs of the human heart, especially in times when life was an agonizing thing.

To study the Canon of Scripture is not to come away with a lesser view of Scripture, but with a far greater view, for it is to see the unanswerable power of the word of God in action in the minds and hearts of men and women.

It is my hope and prayer that, as people read this book, they will come more and more to realize the self-evidencing power of the word of God. All through my own life my experience has been that the more I knew about the Bible, the greater the Bible became, and it is my prayer that the reading of the story of how the Bible came to be what it is today may convince even more those who read it that the Bible is the word of God to all people.

William Barclay

Part I

The Making of the Old Testament

TO THE JEWS the Scriptures were indeed the Holy
Scriptures. They expressed this special holiness in a very
curious way. 'All the Holy Scriptures,' says the *Mishnah,*
'render the hands unclean' (Yadaim 3:5). When a man had
touched an unclean thing he had to go through a process
of the most meticulous cleansing and washing of his
hands to remove all possible defilement. The law was that
he must do exactly the same after he had touched any of
the rolls which contained the books of Scripture. The
intention of that strange regulation was to make it very
difficult to handle the rolls of Scripture at all; they were
so holy that they must be fenced about with rules and
regulations which made it difficult even to take them
within the hands.

The process by which the Old Testament came to
contain the books which it does today is a long story. It
began with the emergence of the Book of Deuteronomy in
621 BC and finished with the decisions of the Council of
Jamnia in AD 90 or thereby. It took seven hundred years
and more to build up the divine library of the Old Testament; and it is the story of that long process which we
are to study.

The Three Sections

As the Jews regarded it, the Old Testament fell into three
sections—the Law, the Prophets and the Writings, *ie* the

Torah, the *Nebiim*, and the *Kethubim*. That division goes at least as far back as about 180 BC, when the Greek translation of *Ecclesiasticus* was made. The original author of the Hebrew version of that book was Jesus ben Sirach, and the Greek version was made by his grandson. In the Prologue to the Greek translation the grandson speaks of the many good things which were given to Israel for wisdom and instruction by the Law, the Prophets, and by the others who followed in their steps; and he tells how his grandfather gave a lot of his time to the reading of the law and the prophets and the other books of our fathers.

These are the earliest references to the threefold division of Scripture which became so familiar to the Jews.

The Law consisted of the first five books of the Old Testament—Genesis, Exodus, Leviticus, Numbers and Deuteronomy.

The Prophets fell into two sections. First, there were 'the Former Prophets', which we regard as historical books —Joshua, Judges, Samuel, and Kings. The last two books were generally, but not always, regarded as two books and not four, as in our reckoning. Second, there were 'the Latter Prophets'—Isaiah, Jeremiah, Ezekiel, and The Twelve. The Twelve, which we sometimes call the Minor Prophets, were reckoned as one book. It ought always to be remembered that when we speak of the 'Minor' Prophets, the word does not imply any kind of inferiority in wisdom or quality or authority, but simply means that the books of these twelve prophets were *shorter* than the books of the great prophets.

The Writings were a much more miscellaneous and loosely connected group, and were composed of Psalms, Proverbs, Job, Ecclesiastes, the Song of Solomon, Ruth, Lamentations, Esther, Ezra-Nehemiah, Chronicles, Daniel. Of these eleven books, five were known in particular as the *Five Rolls* because they were specially connected with

2

certain great Jewish festivals at which they were always read. The Song of Solomon was read at the Passover, and allegorically interpreted to tell of the exodus from Egypt. Ruth, the harvest idyll, was read at the Feast of Weeks, which was a harvest-thanksgiving festival. Lamentations was read on the ninth day of the month Ab, which was the day of fasting in memory of the destruction of the Temple. Ecclesiastes was read at the Feast of Tabernacles, because, 'it preaches a thankful enjoyment of life, united with God and consecrated by the fear of God, as the ultimate aim of wisdom' (Cornill). Esther was read at the Festival of Purim, for the existence of which it was the warrant and authority.

Jewish practice did not enumerate the books as we do, nor did it always enumerate them in the same way. The most common method of enumeration, which is usual in the *Talmud*, is to number the books as twenty-four. In the *Talmud* the Old Testament is frequently called the *twenty-four holy Scriptures*, or the *twenty-four books*. In 4 Ezra (2 Esdras), an apocryphal book written towards the end of the first century AD, there is an imaginary story of how Ezra the scribe restored from memory the books of Scripture, when they had been lost, and how he received other books from God along with them; and the story finishes with God's command: 'The twenty-four books that thou hast written publish, that the worthy and unworthy may read therein; but the seventy last thou shalt keep, to deliver them to the wise among the people' (4 Ezra 14:45, 46). The twenty-four books were made up exactly according to the list that we have already given—five books of the Law, four books of the Former Prophets and four books of the Latter Prophets, and eleven books of the Writings. This may be said to be what we might call the official enumeration.

The Grandeur of the Law

Although the Jews regarded all these books as sacred and holy, they did not give to all of them quite the same place. It was in the Law that the greatness of Scripture reached its full height and grandeur. It was the Law which was Scripture *par excellence*. Using the layout of the Temple as a parallel, they said that the Writings were like the Outer Court; the Prophets were like the Holy Place; but the Law was the Holy of Holies. The Law, they said, was created one thousand generations before Moses, and nine hundred and seventy-four generations before the creation of the world, and was, therefore, older than the world itself. When the Messiah came, they said, the Prophets and the Writings would be abrogated, but the Law should endure for ever and ever. The Law, they said, was delivered to Moses by God complete and entire, and he who said that Moses himself wrote even one letter of it was guilty of sin; it was literally and completely the word of God.

Jewish boys were taught the Law from their first consciousness, and had these laws, as it were, 'engraven on their souls' (Josephus, *Against Apion*, 2:18). They learn them from their earliest youth, so that 'they bear the image of the laws in their souls' (Philo, *Embassy to Caius*, 31). From their swaddling-clothes they were instructed in these sacred laws (Philo, *Embassy to Caius*, 31). The Jew might in his national misfortunes lose everything, but he could not lose the Law; and however far from his native land he was, and however hostile a ruler might be, he feared the Law more than any man (Josephus, *Against Apion*, 2:38). History was full of examples of Jews who had chosen to die rather than be disloyal to, or abandon, or disobey the Law (Josephus, *Against Apion*, 1:8). In the Law the very being and essence of Scripture was concentrated. Great as the Prophets and the Writings might be, they were only *quabbalah*, tradition, explanation, or interpretation of the Law. It is, therefore, with the story of the canonization of the Law that we must begin.

When we make a careful study of the Law, the first five books of the Old Testament, the *Pentateuch* (which means the five rolls) we come to see that it is a composite document, and that it must have been the product of a long growth and development. Jewish tradition ascribed every word of it to Moses, but there are clear signs that others besides Moses must have had a hand in its writing. Deuteronomy 34 tells of the death of Moses—a story which Moses himself could hardly have written. Genesis 36 gives a list of the kings of Edom, and then says that all these reigned before Israel had a king, which takes us down to the days of Saul at least (Genesis 36:31). Genesis 14:14 tells us that Abram pursued those who had taken Lot captive as far as Dan, but from Judges 18:29 we find that Dan did not receive its name until long after Moses was dead. We find in the Pentateuch repeated references to the Philistines (Genesis 21:34; 26:14-18; Exodus 13:17), and the Philistines did not come into Palestine until about 1200 BC, long after the time of Moses. There are quite certainly sections of the Pentateuch which come from a time long after Moses.

Further, we find that the Pentateuch contains differing accounts of the same incident. There are, for instance, two stories of how Beersheba got its name, one tracing it back to a covenant between Abraham and Abimelech, the other to an incident in the relationships between Isaac and Abimelech (Genesis 21:31; 26:31). There are two stories of how Bethel got its name, the one tracing it back to the vision of Jacob on the way to Pandanaram, the other to an incident years later when Jacob was returning from Pandanaram (Genesis 28:19; 35:15).

These are small points, but often the difference is more important. There are two distinct accounts of the banishment of Hagar. In the one she is banished before her child Ishmael has grown into a lad (Genesis 16:6*ff*; 21:9*ff*). Still more important, there are two quite distinct accounts of the creation story. In Genesis 1 man and woman are created at the end of creation after all the animals and the rest of the world have been formed. In Genesis 2 man is created first, then the animals and finally woman. There are two quite distinct accounts of the Flood story. In the one Noah is commanded to take into the ark two of every beast (Genesis 6:19), in the other seven of each clean animal and two of each unclean (7:2), a difference which is underlined when the narrative goes on to say that all the animals went into the ark in pairs (7:8, 9). It is clear that in these stories the men who put the Pentateuch into its final form found two accounts of these incidents and events, and with complete honesty and fidelity to their sources they included both.

Perhaps most surprising of all is the difference in the use of the name of God. To see this clearly we must note that when the Authorized Version (AV) uses the word LORD in capital letters, it is translating Jehovah in the original Hebrew. In Exodus 6:2 we see God encouraging Moses in his contest with Pharaoh. 'God spake unto Moses and said unto him: I am the LORD; and I appeared unto Abraham, unto Isaac, and unto Jacob, by the name of God Almighty, but by my name Jehovah was I not know to them.' And yet in Genesis 15:2 and 8, we find Abraham calling God by the name Jehovah. We find both Sarah and Laban using that name (Genesis 16:2; 24:31). We find the name used in the days of Seth (Genesis 4:26); and we even find Eve using the name Jehovah when she had borne a child (Genesis 4:1). There is quite clearly more than one source here, and to note these discrepancies is not in the least to belittle or criticize the compilers of the Pentateuch; it is rather to underline the meticulous honesty with which they dealt with the sources and documents with which they worked.

We must now go on to see the process by which the Law grew up, and by which it came to be accepted by the Jews as the very word of God.

To the Jews God was characteristically a self-revealing God. According to G F Moore, the outstanding characteristic of Judaism is that it conceived of itself as a *revealed* religion. God, as the Jews thought of him, is a God who desires to make himself and his will known to men, and who continually takes steps to bring that knowledge to men. The natural result of this point of view is that in Judaism the supreme figure is the *prophet*, who is the messenger of God to men, and it is through the prophet that the revelation of God to men is commonly made. The promise made through Moses is that God will always give to the nation a prophet (Deuteronomy 18:15). The claim of Amos is that God does nothing without revealing his secret to his servants the prophets (Amos 3:7). God by his Spirit sent his word to men in the prophets, and it was the sin of the nation that men refused to hear (Zechariah 7:12). That is why Judaism ranked all the great national figures as prophets. Abraham, Isaac, Jacob, David, Job, Ezra, Mordecai were all prophets; the Jewish scholars enumerated forty-eight prophets and seven prophetesses in their national history. This means that the revelation of God was conceived of as essentially a *spoken* revelation. God spoke to the prophets, and then the prophets spoke to men. The question then is, in a world of religious thought in which the supreme figures were inspired *men,* how did the idea of an inspired *book* emerge? 'How did the Israelites come to believe that God not only spoke but also dictated a book?' (Pfieffer).

7

The Starting-Point of Scripture

It is just here that we are fortunate enough to have a fixed date which is a starting-point for the whole idea of canonization and of sacred Scripture. It is to be understood that what follows is a reconstruction of events, as we think that they happened, and, although in our narrative we state the events as facts, we are none the less well aware that it is reconstruction and not indubitable history which we are presenting. In the year 621 BC a book which can only have been the Book of Deuteronomy was discovered in the Temple (2 Kings 22:8-20). At the time the young Josiah was king, and he was a good king, and a true seeker after God. This book which had been discovered was accepted as the word of God, and was deliberately taken as nothing less than the law of the nation (2 Kings 23:3). Here is the beginning of the whole process. A book has been accepted as the revealed word of God, and it has been openly and deliberately and publicly taken as the law of the nation and of the individual. 'For the first time in the history of mankind, a book was canonized as sacred scripture' (Pfeiffer).

But we must follow the process further. The publication of Deuteronomy very naturally stimulated the interest in written books, and there was another great book lying ready to hand. This was a great epic story which told of the history of Israel down to the death of David, and which was itself a compilation which had been made somewhere about 650 BC. To this document has been given the name of 'JE', because it is formed by the coming together of two documents called respectively J and E. These documents have been given these identifying initials because one of them calls God by the name *Jehovah* right from the beginning, while the other calls God by the name *Elohim*, which is the general Hebrew word used for God until the revelation of the name of Jehovah to Moses in Exodus 3:11-18. It is precisely because these two documents have been put together that there were the discrepancies which exist in certain sections of the Pentateuch.

Some Discrepancies

As a brief illustration of this, let us look at the discrepancies which we noted in the Flood story. In Genesis 6:19 Noah is bidden to take two animals of every kind, and we note that this instruction occurs in a passage in which the speaker is God, that is *Elohim* (Genesis 6:13). In Genesis 7:2 there is the instruction to take sevens of the clean beasts and two of the unclean beasts and we note that this instruction occurs in a passage in which the speaker is the LORD, that is, *Jehovah* (Genesis 7:1). Further we note that the passage which says that the beasts went into the ark two by two is a passage in which the divine name is God, that is *Elohim* (Genesis 7:9). This is an illustration of how the two documents were put together, and how in their earlier sections they can be distinguished by the name of God which each of them uses.

J, the document which calls God Jehovah from the very beginning, is one of the supreme religious documents of the world's literature. In the words of H H Rowley, 'The literary genius of its author will make it live, if only as literature, so long as men read literature'. It thinks and speaks of God with a lovely childlike simplicity. Jehovah makes man from the dust of the earth and breathes life into his nostrils (2:7). He makes woman, man's partner, from a rib taken from man (2:22). Jehovah plants a garden and walks in it in the cool of the day (3:8). When Noah has embarked his cargo and himself safely into the Ark, Jehovah shuts the door after him (7:16). There has never

9

been any book which has spoken with such a lovely, childlike simplicity about God. When we further study this document called J, we find that it is specially interested in Judah and in the Southern Kingdom of Israel. It is in Hebron that Abraham dwells, and it is to Hebron that the spies go when they enter the land, and in the story of Joseph it is Judah who is the leading figure. We, therefore, may say that this document is the document which was produced in the land of Judah and in the Southern Kingdom to tell of the early history of Israel.

The document which is called E, as we have seen, does not call God Jehovah until after the revelation of that name to Moses. That is why in the Pentateuch we find one line of thought which says that although Abraham and the patriarchs knew God, they did not know him by his name Jehovah, and another line of thought in which the name Jehovah is used from the days of Eve. E does not begin with creation: it begins with Abraham. It is not so simple and childlike as J is; it is specially interested in dreams and angels and in blessings and farewells. When we study it, we find that it is specially interested in Northern Israel. In its version of the Joseph story it is Reuben who plays the leading part. In the time of the Exodus it gives special prominence to Joshua who was from Ephraim; and in the Jacob story the centres are Bethel and Shechem. We, therefore, may say that this document is the document which was produced in the Northern Kingdom to tell of the early history of Israel. It is convenient for memory to make the letters J and E stand not only for Jehovah and Elohim, but also for Judah and Ephraim, so that they may also remind us of the parts of Israel from which these two documents came.

So, then, when Deuteronomy emerged, the Israelites already possessed the incomparable epic history contained in JE; and since Deuteronomy was taken to be the work of

Moses, it was amalgamated with JE, and inserted in the narrative before the death of Moses. Thus slowly the Pentateuch was being built up, and the divine library was taking its first steps to growth.

The Holiness Code

Now there follows still another addition. The great basic sentence which in itself contains the very essence of the religion of Israel is: 'Ye shall be holy, for I Jehovah your God am holy' (Leviticus 19:2). Bit by bit there had grown up rules and regulations and principles governing this holiness, and laying down in what this holiness consists. These holiness laws are embodied in a document which is known as the *Holiness Code*, which is contained in Leviticus 17-26, and which is usually denoted by the letter H. This was compiled and published somewhere about 550 BC, and it was natural that it, too, should be added to the growing sacred literature of Israel. So then, the Holiness Code was, as it were, the next volume to be added to the divine library of the Old Testament.

There remains one great volume to be added, and then the Pentateuch is complete. This last section of the Pentateuch is called P, because it contains all the great ritual and sacrificial practice in the second Temple, and it is essentially a priestly document. It is composed of the remaining part of Leviticus, in which the sacrificial laws are set out. It also contains the rest of the history of the Pentateuch, and it is characterized by certain features. It can be novel and austere, as it is in Genesis 1, when it tells its story of creation. It often tells stories to explain how the great religious practices and festivals of Israel came into being. For instance, its creation story explains the supreme importance of the Sabbath day. It is very fond of genealogies—to a priest purity of lineage was essential

11

—and the long genealogies of the Pentateuch belong to it. And it became the great framework into which all the other parts of the Pentateuch were fitted. It was completed somewhere around 500 BC.

So at last, after more than a century under the guidance of the Spirit of God, the great divine library of the Pentateuch stood complete. It had begun with Deuteronomy; it had embraced the precious history of J and E; it had taken in the great Holiness Code; and finally it had found its unity in the setting of the laws and the history of the great priestly document called P. To put it briefly, we might say that the Law—the Pentateuch—equals D + JE + H + P.

But we must now ask, when did this great document become sacred Scripture? When did it cease to be simply a great and precious book, and when did it come to be regarded and accepted as, in a special and unique sense, nothing less than, and nothing other than, the word of God?

A first step was that the part of it which told specially of the great laws of Israel became separated from the rest. That is to say, the Law proper—the first five books of the Bible—became separated from Joshua, Judges, Samuel and Kings. It was the Law of God which was of supreme importance. Three things help us fix a time when the Law became Scripture in the full sense of the term:

(1) One of the great events in religious history was when the Old Testament was translated into Greek, and when the Greek Old Testament, which is known as the *Septuagint*, and which is denoted by the letters LXX, first emerged. This was important because it now meant that the Old Testament was no longer hidden away in the Hebrew language, but became available to almost the whole world, for at that time almost all men spoke Greek as well as their own tongue. That translation was made under the auspices of Ptolemy the Second Philadelphus,

who was king of Egypt from 285-246 BC. It was originally only the Law which was translated, and we know that by this time the Law was *par excellence* the sacred book of the Jews. It was for them Scripture in the full sense of the term. We can then say with certainty that by 250 BC the Law was Scripture. But can we trace the story back even further?

(2) To this day the Samaritans accept only the Pentateuch as Scripture, and do not accept the other books of the Old Testament. This can only mean that when the Samaritans split from the Jews, and when the great national schism took place, the Scriptures consisted only of the Law, for it was only the Law that the Samaritans took with them. When that great and lasting schism took place is not accurately certain, but there is good evidence to suggest that it began to threaten in the days of Nehemiah at least, that is, at some time not very long before 400 BC.

(3) Finally, in Nehemiah 8-10 we have the story of Ezra, the scribe, reading the sacred book of the Law to the assembled people. We need not take that story absolutely literally, but what we can say is this: when the people returned from exile under Ezra and Nehemiah, it must have become clear to them that political greatness was not for them. They, therefore, chose to find their greatness in religion and in spiritual things and it was then that Israel became in a unique and special sense The People of the Book.

Everything points to the probability that the Law acquired the status of fully sacred Scripture, that it became in a special sense the binding word of God for Israel, in the time of Ezra and Nehemiah, that is, about 400 BC.

So then, by 400 BC the first stone in the edifice of Scripture is well and truly laid; the first great volume is deposited in the divine library; the Canon of the Old Testament has begun. By that time the Law (*Torah*) has become Scripture, never to lose its place, to gain through-out the years an ever higher and higher place, a place for ever kept before the eyes of the people, because the Law became the book whose reading was the centre of every Synagogue service.

Other Additions

As the years went on other books were to be added to the divine library, but no book was ever to be on a level with the Law; the Law was to stand in Judaism for ever with-out an equal or even a rival.

Whatever else was to be added to the Jewish Scrip-tures in the days to come, the Law stood alone in all the splendour of the fulness of its revelation.

The Prophets

But something was added to the divine library of Scripture. The Old Testament has a second part, and that part is the Prophets. We must now go on to see how that part of it became canonical. There is a sense in which the Law could not stand alone. If it sought to, it lacked that very thing which gave it birth—prophecy. It was the prophets who had been God's messengers to men, and who had been the guides and the directors of the nation, who had moved the people to walk in the ways of God and had warned and restrained them when they went astray. Without prophecy 'the Law was a body without a soul' (Dillman). As we shall see, it was the conviction of the Jews that with Malachi, midway through the fifth century BC, the voice of prophecy had fallen for ever silent, for 'it needed more than the Law to fill the gap' (Ryle).

We must first remind ourselves of what the Prophets

are composed. They were composed of the *Former Prophets,* which are the books of Joshua, Judges, Samuel, and Kings, and of the *Latter Prophets,* which are composed of Isaiah, Jeremiah, Ezekiel, and The Twelve.

To us it seems strange to find Joshua, Judges, Samuel, and Kings classed as prophetic books. There is more than one explanation for their inclusion. It is suggested that they are thought to be prophetic because they tell of the works and words of the oldest prophets, of men like Samuel, Nathan, Ahijah, and above all, Elijah and Elisha.

According to Jewish tradition these books were written by prophets. Joshua himself is said to have written the book which bears his name. Samuel is said to have written Judges and Samuel. Jeremiah is said to be the author of Kings. But the truth is that, although these books are apparently history books, their real aim and function is to set out the principles of the prophets in action. H H Rowley reminds us that to the Hebrew the will of God always became known through concrete experience. These books proclaim the prophetic principles as clearly as the prophets did, for their one aim is to show in every incident which they relate that the way of wisdom and happiness and prosperity lies in obedience to God, and disobedience to God is the inevitable way to disaster. These books are not history books; they are demonstrations of prophetic truth in action. The writers were not annalists interested in events as such; they were interested in events only as the working out and the demonstration of the will of God. They are concerned to depict history as the action of God, and to show that the words of the prophets, warnings and promises alike, are true.

There were many reasons why the canonization of these books was natural and inevitable:

They had already existed for many generations, for many of the prophets had committed their words to writing.

'Bind up the testimony, seal the law among my disciples,' said Isaiah (8:16), and Ezekiel knew and quoted the words which God had spoken by his former prophets (Ezekiel 38:17). Throughout the years these prophetic books had been the devotional literature of the devout in Israel. These were not books which had their place to make: their place *was* made, and they were already enthroned within the hearts of men.

It was during the dark days of the exile in distant Babylon that the prophets became indispensable to the heart of a devout Jew. These were days of national disaster. What more natural than that a Jew should turn to the prophets?

'The deportation [to Babylon] itself would necessarily present itself to the people in the light of a fulfilment of the prophetic warnings. Now they searched the same oracles, which their fathers had spurned, for light in the darkness. If these had proved themselves truthful in their presages of punishment, they would also in Yahwe's time prove themselves faithful in their predictions of a blessed future.'   (*Wildeboer*)

'In the time of the Exile, when the national existence with which the ancient religion of Israel was so closely intertwined was hopelessly shattered, when the voice of the prophets was stilled, and the public services of the sanctuary no longer called the devout together, the whole continuance of the spiritual faith rested upon the remembrance that the prophets of the Lord had foreseen the catastrophe, and had shown how to reconcile it with undiminished trust in Jehovah, the God of Israel.'

(*Robertson Smith*)

They became 'the main support of the faithful, who felt, as they have never felt before, that the words of Jehovah were pure words, silver sevenfold tried, a sure treasure in every time of need'. Even when they returned from exile these older books were a necessary stay and support, for even then their condition was wretched in the extreme. So they read eagerly the story of the ancient and the glorious days. They knew that their sufferings had been caused by their sin, and in the history of the Former Prophets and the promises of the Latter Prophets they gained the certainty that, if they walked in the ways of God, the great days would come again. In the days of the Exile and the return, the Prophets had been the food on which men fed their fainting souls. So in the circumstances of the Exile and the troubled days of the return, the Prophets became to men the very word of God.

There was another factor in the situation which was significant and influential. It was fixed Jewish belief that with Malachi, midway through the fifth century BC, the voice of prophecy was silenced and never spoke again.

There are signs of this belief even within the Old Testament itself. In Deuteronomy the hope and the belief is that God will always raise up a prophet for his people (Deuteronomy 18:15) but in Malachi all that can be expected is not the emergence of any new prophet, but the return of Elijah (Malachi 4:5). Zechariah envisages a time when anyone who claims to be a prophet must be necessarily an impostor. 'If anyone again appears as a prophet, his father and mother who bore him will say to him, You shall not live, for you speak lies in the name of the Lord; and his father and mother who bore him shall pierce him through when he prophesies' (Zechariah 13:3). In Psalm 74 there is a verse which is probably not a part of the original psalm but rather a comment of some editor, and it is a verse of this latter-day despair: 'There is no longer any prophet and there is none among us who knows how long' (Psalm 74:9).

In 1 Maccabees we repeatedly come upon this belief. That book speaks of a sorrow in Israel 'such as there has not been since the days that the prophets ceased to appear among them' (1 Maccabees 4:46). It tells that they agreed to make Simon high priest until such time as a prophet should appear (1 Maccabees 14:41).

It is the same in the writings of the Rabbis. One passage says that up until Alexander the Great—Ezra was not very long before Alexander—the prophets prophesied through the Holy Spirit, but from that time onward all that a man could do was to listen to the wise, that is, to the scribes. Rabbi Akiba, writing in the Christian era, declared that any Jew who read in the Christian books had no share in the life to come. He went on to say that books, like that of Ben Sirah and others, which had been composed after the age of the prophets had closed, might be read, but only as a man reads a letter.

Just because the days of the prophets were held to have ended with Haggai and Zechariah and Malachi, the works of the great prophets were of extreme preciousness. They belonged to an age of inspiration which no longer existed. The 'Thus saith the Lord' of the prophets was something that a man could never hope to hear again. In view of that fact it was only natural that the works of the great prophets should be lovingly collected, and carefully preserved, and diligently studied. The very fact that men were conscious of living in an age of lesser inspiration gave to the great prophets a new place in life and thought. We must now go on to ask when the works of the prophets were collected and edited and issued.

Here we are in the realm of tradition and legend, but even in the case of legend and tradition it may be possible to penetrate to the truth which lies behind them. There are three main lines of such legends which we must take into account.

(1) 2 Maccabees begins with a letter which is certainly a work of fiction. In that letter there is a statement about Nehemiah. It says of him that he founded a library, 'and gathered together the acts of the kings, and the prophets, and of David, and the epistles of the kings concerning the holy gifts and sacrifices' (2 Maccabees 2:13). It is hard to say what, if any, truth lies behind this; but in this statement Nehemiah is credited with collecting the prophetic writings.

(2) Jewish belief always gave Ezra an all-important place in the formation of the Old Testament. The Talmud says of him that he would have been worthy enough for the Torah to have been given to Israel through his hand, if Moses had not preceded him. The legend comes to its peak in the apocryphal book known as 2 Esdras, which belongs to the latter part of the first century AD. According to that book the Law was lost and burned in the national disasters. Ezra prayed to God that he might be enabled to write down all that God had done in history, and all that God was still to do, as it had been written in the Law. He was told to withdraw from men for forty days, taking five skilful penmen with him. He was given a cup to drink, and he spoke continuously for forty days and nights. In that time ninety-four books were produced, seventy of which were to be handed over to the wise, and twenty-four which were to be published for all to read, and these twenty-four were the canonical books of the Old Testament (4 Ezra 14:19-48). Once again this is pure legend, but it ascribes to Ezra the preservation and the promulgation of the whole Old Testament.

(3) In Jewish tradition we meet with a body called The Great Synagogue. In the *Sayings of the Fathers* we read that, 'Moses received the *Torah* from Sinai and del-

ivered it to Joshua, and Joshua to the elders, and the elders to the prophets, and the prophets to the men of the Great Synagogue'. This Great Synagogue was said to have been a body of men convened by Ezra and numbering one hundred and twenty, and including, amongst others, Haggai, Zechariah, Malachi, Nehemiah, Daniel and Mordecai. The Great Synagogue was the spiritual ruler of Israel. It is said that the men of the Great Synagogue wrote Ezekiel, the Book of the Twelve Prophets, Daniel, and Esther, and that at the same time Ezra wrote the book which bears his name, and the genealogies in Chronicles up to his own time.

However, if we say that the Great Synagogue *edited* and *published* these books rather than *wrote* them we will come near to the meaning of this tradition. Once again we are in the realm of legend, and it is very doubtful if the Great Synagogue ever existed at all.

The Prophets Established

Jewish traditional and legendary accounts lay down very definitely that the books of Scripture were assembled and collected and even canonized in the days of Ezra and Nehemiah. It may well be that none of these legends and traditions is anything like accurate history, but it seems to us certain that they do preserve the memory of the fact that it was in the days of Ezra and Nehemiah that the Law became canonical and that the Prophets were assembled and collected. Throughout the exile, men had fed their souls on the Prophets. In the deep disappointments and the heart-breaking problems of the return, they had found their help and their support in the prophetic writings; and it was then that the prophetic writings were deliberately collected and preserved. It is to be noted that at this stage it is not a matter of declaring the prophets sacred Scripture,

20

and not a matter of placing them in the Canon beside the Law; it is still a matter of collecting well-loved books, and ensuring that they will never get lost. Canonization was still to come. Have we any indication as to when it did come?

We may begin our investigation with one pointer which provides us with a date at which the Prophets were almost certainly regarded as canonical and as Holy Scripture. The Book of Daniel appeared about 165 BC. Now Daniel is quite clearly a prophetic book and yet never at any time did it appear amongst the prophets, and always it was included among the Writings. This can only mean that by the time Daniel appeared the number of the prophets was closed; the prophetic literature was a fixed and settled body into which no other book, however well qualified, could find an entry. It is safe to say that means that the Prophets were regarded as Holy Scripture at least by the time of Daniel in 165 BC.

So then, by the beginning of the second century BC, a further stone has been added to the edifice of Scripture; a further section has been added to the divine library of the Old Testament, and now beside the Law there stand the Prophets.

At this point a rather significant fact becomes apparent. At no time did there ever arise among the Jews any question or any dispute in regard to any part of the Law. It was unquestionably and unarguably divine from beginning to end. But among the prophets two books came under discussion. The first was Jonah, which was described as 'a book by itself', and which was questioned because it has to do exclusively with the heathen and does not mention Israel at all. To some of the Jewish scholars it seemed strange that a book which, as they saw it, had nothing to do with Israel had a place within the Canon of Israel. They failed to see that in many ways Jonah is the greatest book in the Old Testament, because it lays down the missionary task of Israel as no other book does. The other book which was questioned was the Book of Ezekiel. It was never suggested that Ezekiel should be ejected from the Canon, but it was argued sometimes that Ezekiel should be 'put away', that is, that it should be withdrawn from general circulation, and that it should not be read in the Synagogue. That was due to two things: to the difficulty of the beginning; and the difficulty of the end, especially the passage about the chariot of God.

It was not that anyone wished to eliminate either Jonah or Ezekiel from the Canon of Scripture. It was simply felt that they raised difficulties and the difficulties were openly discussed; and it must be noted that, although that could happen with the Prophets, it could never happen with the Law, which was so divine that it was beyond question and beyond discussion.

The Writings

We have now arrived at the third part of the Old Testament, the part which was known as the *Writings* or the *Hagiographa*. In the case of the *Writings* the story is much less simple and much less straightforward. The Writings do not form a homogeneous whole like the Law or the Prophets. They are rather what has been called 'a miscellany of independent books'. They did not enter the Canon of Scripture as a whole as the Law and the Prophets did, but one by one they came to be regarded as sacred Scripture, rather by popular acceptance than by official decision. For a long time they were not so much Scripture as 'religious literature'. They were not intended to be used, and they were not as a whole used, for public liturgical reading at the worship and service of the Synagogue; they were rather meant for homiletic exposition. They formed what Ryle calls 'an informal appendix to the Law and the Prophets'.

Their secondary quality can be observed in the fact that to the end of the day the Old Testament was commonly referred to as *The Law and the Prophets*. In the preface to Daniel, Jerome writes: 'All Sacred Scripture is divided by them [that is, the Jews] into three parts, into the Law, the Prophets and the Hagiographa'. That is true, but it none the less remains true that Scripture was commonly called *The Law and the Prophets*. We need go no further than the New Testament for abundant evidence of this. 'Think not,' said Jesus, 'that I am come to destroy the Law or the Prophets' (Matthew 5:17). The Golden Rule that we should do to others as we would have them do to us is the essence and summation of the Law and the Prophets (Matthew 7:12). The Law and the Prophets existed until John; thereafter it is the time of the Kingdom (Luke 16:16). It was from Moses and all the Prophets that Jesus expounded the Scriptures (Luke 24:27). In the Synagogue in Antioch in Pisidia, it is the Law and the Prophets which are read (Acts 13:15). In every Synagogue on every Sabbath day, Moses is read (Acts 15:21). It was from the Prophet Isaiah that Jesus read in the Synagogue at Nazareth (Luke 4:17). It was the Law and the Prophets which were read at the public worship of the Synagogue, and it is as the Law and the Prophets that the Old Testament is commonly described. Obviously the Writings, the Hagiographa, do not stand on this same level.

In the same passage as we have quoted above, Jerome goes on to say that there are five books of the Law, eight of the Prophets, and eleven of the Writings. The eleven books of the Writings do not fall into any natural and inevitable sections, and they were divided in different ways:

There were three books of poetry: Psalms, Proverbs, and Job;

Five rolls, *ie* the *Megilloth*, which were, as we shall see, specially connected with five great national occasions: the Song of Solomon, Ruth, Lamentations, Ecclesiastes, and Esther;

One book of prophecy: Daniel;

And two books of history: Ezra-Nehemiah and Chronicles.

Sometimes, as the prophets were, they were divided into the *Former Writings*—the *Rishonim*—*ie* Ruth, Psalms, Job, and Proverbs; and the *Latter Writings*—the *Acharonim*—*ie* Daniel, Ezra-Nehemiah and Chronicles; and the five *Megilloth*.

Sometimes they were divided into the *Major Writings*: Psalms, Job and Proverbs; and the *Minor Writings*: the Song of Solomon, Ecclesiastes and Lamentations; and the *Latter Writings*: Esther, Daniel, Ezra-Nehemiah, Chronicles.

As you can see, they are a highly varied miscellany falling into highly varied sections. Our task is to trace how these eleven books became part of the sacred literature of Israel, and part of the Old Testament.

We may begin with certain general facts:

In the ancient world a book had to be popular and had to be read before it could even survive. We are thinking of an age when books were not printed, but when each copy had to be made by hand; and, if a book was not popular enough to be read, it simply ceased to be copied, and vanished out of existence. These Writings must, therefore, in the first place have been popular works, known and read widely by the ordinary people.

Second, it became a first principle of the Jewish view of sacred books that a book had to be written in Hebrew to be Scripture—or at least in Aramaic—and, if it dealt with history, the history must be the history of the great classical period of the Hebrew story.

Attributed Authorship

Third, we will remember that it was the Jewish conviction that all true prophetic inspiration had ceased with Malachi, and that since about 450 BC the divine voice was silent. At first sight it would, therefore, appear that any book must be written prior to Ezra to have even a chance of entering into the Canon. But there is one extremely interesting exception to that. If a book was anonymous, if no one knew who had written it, and if it had become a book dear to the hearts and minds of people, it was possible that it could be attributed to one of the great figures of the past, and, therefore, could become canonical. That it to say, if a book's author was known to be after Ezra, it had no hope of becoming canonical.

That is what turned the scale against Ecclesiasticus (in the Apocrypha). There are few who would care to deny that Ecclesiasticus is a very great book, and that it is greater in moral and spiritual power than certain books which gained an entry into the Canon, but it never had any hope of entry, because its author was known to be a man called Jesus ben Sirach who had lived not long after 200 BC. Many of the Writings were written in the fourth and the third centuries BC, and at least one—Daniel—in the second century BC, but their authors were unknown, they were anonymous, and, therefore, it was possible to attribute them to the great figures of the past, and so to make it possible for them to enter the Canon. So Ruth was ascribed to Samuel, who was traditionally the author of Judges and the books which bear his name. All the Psalms were ascribed to David. Jeremiah was said to have written both Kings and Lamentations. Proverbs and Ecclesiastes were said to be the work of Solomon. Job was assigned to Moses. Ezra and Nehemiah were the works of Ezra, who was so respected that it was said: 'The *Torah* was forgotten by Israel until Ezra went up from Babylon and *re*-established it'. And Ezra had at least a share in the writing of Chronicles. The Song of Solomon might actually be Solomon's, or at least it was held to belong to the time of Hezekiah. Esther was the work, or at least the editing, of the men of the Great Synagogue.

The Writings could only become canonical because, when their supreme value was realized, they were seen to be anonymous, and could, therefore, be held to be the work of men within the period to which inspiration was said to be confined. This is true even in the case of Daniel. It was well known that Daniel had actually emerged about 165 BC, but it was held to be the actual work of Daniel, the great figure of the exile. It was thus that it was possible for these books to become canonical at all.

Establishing 'The Writings'

When did they come to be regarded as Holy Scripture?

The process was a long one. We must begin by returning to the enigmatic statement about Nehemiah in the admittedly spurious letter at the beginning of 2 Maccabees. There it is said that Nehemiah collected into a library the books about the kings and the prophets, and *ta tou Dauid*, which literally means 'the things of David', and which in the context can most naturally mean the books, or the writings, of David (2 Maccabees 2:13). It may be impossible to place much stress or reliance on that statement, but it may mean that Nehemiah began the whole process by the collection of the Psalms—by no means the whole book as we possess it—which go under the name of David.

It is when we come to Ecclesiasticus (now in the Apo-

26

crypha) that the existence of this third division of Scripture becomes quite clear and certain. Writing in or about 132 BC, the grandson of the original writer of Ecclesiasticus, Jesus ben Sirach, wrote a prologue to his Greek translation of his grandfather's book. There he speaks of the great things handed down to us by the Law and the Prophets and *the others who have followed in their steps.* He tells how his grandfather gave himself to the study of the Law and of the Prophets and of *the other books of our fathers.* And he speaks about the Law, the Prophecies, and *the rest of the books.* He does not use the term 'Writings'; he does not define what these other books are. It is clear that they are not nearly so well defined a body of literature as the Law and the Prophets are; but it is also clear that by the second century BC there stands beside the Law and the Prophets a body of literature less well defined than they are, but none the less an essential part of the sacred literature of the Jews.

Our next witness comes from the New Testament itself. In Luke's Gospel we read that the risen Christ told the disciples about the things which must be fulfilled in Him, which were written in the Law of Moses and in the Prophets and in the Psalms (Luke 24:44). Here we see that the Psalms are included in, or perhaps are taken as typical and representative of, a body of sacred literature other than the Law and the Prophets. Once again the existence of the Writings is assured, although their constituent parts are still undefined.

When we come to the end of the first Christian century we can call two much more definite witnesses. We have already seen the tradition that Ezra rewrote the whole of the sacred literature; and in that tradition we read that the books which were to be open to all men numbered twenty-four, which by Jewish reckoning is exactly the same number of books as are in the Old Testament (4 Ezra 14:44-46). 4

Ezra (Apocrypha) was written under Domitian about AD 90, and here we have proof that by that time the list of the books was settled, and, therefore, the number of the Writings must have been as firmly fixed as the number of books in the Law and in the Prophets.

The second witness is Josephus who wrote about AD 100. He says that, unlike the Greeks who have vast numbers of conflicting and mutually contradictory books, the Jews have only twenty-two. He arrives at this number by reckoning Ruth and Judges as one book, and Jeremiah and Lamentations as one book. He goes on to say that there are the five books of Moses, the thirteen books of the Prophets, and four books with hymns or precepts for practical help for life. He arrives at this classification by including Daniel, Job, Chronicles, Ezra-Nehemiah, and Esther with the prophetic books. He then goes on to say:

'There is practical proof of the spirit in which we treat our Scriptures. For although so great an interval of time [since they were written] has now passed, not a soul has ventured either to add, or to remove, or to alter a syllable; and it is the instinct of every Jew, from the day of his birth, to consider these books as the teaching of God, to abide by them, and if need be, cheerfully to lay down his life for them.'

(Josephus, *Against Apion* 1:8)

Here is the proof that by the time of Josephus, the number of books in the Writings was regarded as fixed and unalterable, because the number of books in Scripture was so regarded.

It remains now to see the final step in the actual time process of the making of the Old Testament.

Somewhere about AD 90 at Jamnia, which was also called Jabne, and which was near Jaffa and not far from the sea, an authoritative council of the Jewish Rabbis and scholars met, and at that council the books of the Old Testament were at last finally settled, and the number was laid down as we have it today. From that time forward, although a scholar here or there might express doubts about this or that book amongst the Writings, there was never any real question or argument about the contents of the sacred Scriptures of the Old Testament. The process which had begun with the emergence of Deuteronomy in 621 BC had ended with the Council of Jamnia in AD 90. The divine library of the Old Testament had taken more than seven hundred years to assemble.

The People of the Book

History has a strange way of repeating itself. It was at Jamnia in AD 90 that the Old Testament Canon was finally fixed. And Jamnia came only twenty years after the supreme disaster of Jewish history, the disaster from which the nation never recovered: the destruction of the Temple and the near-obliteration of Jerusalem in AD 70. Once again in the time of disaster it was to the word of God that the nation was driven. With every worldly hope shattered, faced with a future in which humanly speaking they had nothing to hope for, the Jews had to become *the people of the book*, and for that very reason it was then that the book had to be definitely and finally defined. With nothing else left to live for, the Jews began to live for the study of God's word. The Jews clung to the sacred Scriptures not because of any theological theory of inspiration, but because they found in them the comfort of God in their sorrow, the hope of God in their despair, the light of God in their darkness, and the strength of God in a world where for them the foundations were shaken.

It remains briefly to look at the individual books within

the Writings and to see how they fared, and in particular to note which of them had questionings and opposition to face.

To the Book of Psalms there was never any opposition, and doubtless it was the first of all the Writings to fix itself in the hearts of men. It was the hymnbook of the Temple, and the prayerbook of the community, as Cornill described it. The order of the Psalms in the daily worship of the Temple was as follows:

On the first day of the week Psalm 24 was sung—'The earth is the Lord's and the fulness thereof'—in commemoration of the first day of creation, when 'God possessed the world and ruled in it';

On the second day of the week Psalm 48 was sung—'Great is the Lord and greatly to be praised'— because on the second day of creation 'God divided His works and reigned over them';

On the third day of the week Psalm 82 was sung—'God standeth in the creation of the mighty'—because on that day the earth appeared, on which are the Judge and the judged';

On the fourth day of the week Psalm 94 was sung—'O Lord God to whom vengeance belongeth'—'because on the fourth day God made the sun, moon, and stars, and will be avenged on those that worship them';

On the fifth day of the week Psalm 81 was sung—'Sing aloud unto God our strength'—'because of the variety of creatures created that day to praise His name';

On the sixth day Psalm 93 was sung—'The Lord reigneth'—'because on that day God finished His works and made man, and the Lord ruled over all His works';

Lastly, on the seventh day, the Sabbath day, Psalm 92 was sung—'It is a good thing to give thanks to the Lord' —'because the Sabbath is symbolic of the millennial kingdom at the end of the six thousand years dispensation, when the Lord will reign over all, and His glory and service will fill the earth with thanksgiving'.

From the beginning the place of the Psalms was never questioned, for they had a unique place in the public services of the Temple and in the private devotions of the hearts of men.

Certain others of the Writings had their place in public services. The High Priest read in public from Chronicles, Job, Ezra-Nehemiah, and Daniel on the evening before the Day of Atonement. The five *Megilloth*—the word means rolls—were read at the great Jewish festivals. The Song, which was allegorized to symbolize the deliverance from Egypt, was read on the eighth day of the Passover. Ruth, the harvest story, was read on the second day of Pentecost. Lamentations was read on 9th Ab, which was the anniversary of the destruction of Solomon's Temple. Ecclesiastes was read on the third day of the Feast of Tabernacles, to remind men to remember God in the midst of the enjoyment of material blessing. Esther was read at the Feast of Purim, for which it is the warrant. The five *Megilloth* were the only books of the Writings to be read in the Synagogue, and they were read only on their special occasions; and, as we shall see, certain of them were very far from being undisputed.

As we have seen, the place of Psalms was never in doubt. Job, too, was never questioned. Job was attributed to Moses, in accordance with the belief that every prophet described his own period, for Job was taken to belong to the patriarchal age. Ruth and Lamentations were never questioned, because Ruth went with Judges and Lamentations with Jeremiah. Daniel was never questioned, because, in spite of its late emergence, its authorship was ascribed to the great Daniel of the exilic period.

On a few occasions Proverbs was questioned. It was questioned on two grounds. First, that Proverbs contains apparent contradictions. Proverbs 26:4, 5 reads: '*Answer not a fool according to his folly*, lest thou also be like unto him. *Answer a fool according to his folly,* lest he be wise in his own conceit'. Second, it was argued that a passage such as Proverbs 7:7-20 presented ethical problems which were difficult to solve. The argument about Proverbs was never at any time very serious, and it must be remembered that it was never suggested that Proverbs should be discarded, but only that it should be withheld from ordinary people who might be puzzled and even misled by the apparent difficulties and contradictions.

It was with difficulty that Esther gained a final place in the Canon, and even after it had gained its place, as late as the third century there were those who were not happy about it. The straits in which the supporters of Esther found themselves are illustrated by a Rabbinic tradition about the book. It was said that Rabbi Samuel had said that Esther did not defile the hands, that is to say it was not a sacred book. Rabbi Judah in speaking of this tradition said, 'Did Samuel mean that Esther was not spoken by the Holy Spirit? Samuel undoubtedly taught that Esther was spoken by the Holy Spirit, but it was spoken to be recited and not to be written'. Such a statement shows the difficulties which Esther encountered.

The problem with Esther was twofold. First, from beginning to end it never mentions the name of God, a truly extraordinary fact in a sacred book. Second, there was in some ways an even more difficult problem. Esther tells of the foundation of the Feast of Purim, and it was at the Feast of Purim that Esther was read in the Synagogue. Now the trouble was that the Feast of Purim is a Feast which finds no warrant and no justification in the Mosaic Law, and the Mosaic Law was taken as a first principle to be absolutely complete (Leviticus 27:34). Here, indeed, was a difficulty. It was circumvented by the tradition that although the instructions for the Feast of Purim are not written down in the Law, they were nevertheless given to Moses by God verbally during the forty days and forty nights on the mountain, but were not written down until the days of Mordecai. However the fact remained that for long Esther was in dispute, and some have always doubted its right to a place in the Canon of Holy Scripture.

Serious controversy in regard to the Writings also centred round two books—Ecclesiastes and the Song. Not unnaturally the weary pessimism of Ecclesiastes and the fact that the Song is one of the world's great love poems, which has to be allegorized to become a religious book at all, presented problems.

It may be said that Esther, Ecclesiastes and the Song were the books which were the most controversial, for even after the Council of Jamnia there were those who were unwilling to accept them; and it is significant that these are three of the very few Old Testament books which are never quoted or referred to in the New Testament.

The Emergence of Sacred Scripture

This then is the story of the building up over seven hundred years of the divine library of the Old Testament.

From this story one thing stands out with unmistakable clarity. It was in the dark days of the Exile that men discovered the Prophets as the word of God. It was in the agony of the time of Antiochus Epiphanes that the Writings began to emerge as sacred Scripture. It was when life had taken everything else away that the Jewish scholars at the Council of Jamnia defined the content of Scripture, accepted the fact that Israel was the People of the Book, and dedicated their lives to the study of the word of God. Here is no human work. The books of the Old Testament took their place as sacred Scripture, not because of the *fiat* or decision of any council or committee of the Church, but because history and experience had manifestly and effectively demonstrated them *to be* the word of God. These were the books in which men had met God in the times which tried men's souls, and in which they had discovered the strength and the comfort of the Almighty. When any council gave any decision in regard to any book or books of the Old Testament, it was simply repeating and affirming proven experience. Such councils did not make these books into sacred Scripture and into the word of God; they simply recorded the fact that men had already found them thus.

And in these books men continued to find God. There have always been times from Marcion onwards when men wished to lay aside the Old Testament as outdated and outworn. One of the extraordinary features of the early Church is the number of men who were converted by reading the Old Testament. Tatian tells us how he was initiated into the Mysteries and how he had tried all that heathen religion and philosophy had to offer, and had come away empty. Then he goes on to say:

> 'I happened to meet with certain barbaric writings, too old to be compared with the opinions of the Greeks, and too divine to be compared with their errors; and I was led to put faith in these by the unpretending cast of the language, the inartificial character of the writers, the foreknowledge displayed of future events, the excellent quality of the precepts, and the declaration of the government of the universe as being centred in one Being'.

(Tatian, *Address to the Greeks* 29)

These writings were the writings of the prophets and in them Tatian found the voice of God. Theophilus of Antioch tells us of his vain search for God. 'At the same time,' he says, 'I met with the sacred Scriptures of the holy prophets,' and it was through them that he was led to God (Theophilus, *To Autolycus* 1:14). And Justin Martyr said:

> 'There existed long before this time certain men more ancient than all those who are esteemed philosophers, both righteous and beloved by God, who spoke by the divine Spirit, and foretold events which would take place, and which are now taking place. They are called prophets. These alone both saw and announced the truth to men, neither reverencing, nor fearing any man, not influenced by a desire for glory, but speaking those things alone which they saw and heard, being filled with the Holy Spirit.'   (*Dialogue with Trypho* 7)

Athenagoras, presenting his plea for the Christians to the Emperor Marcus Aurelius and his colleague Lucius Aurelius Commodus, actually said to them:'I expect that you who are so learned and so eager for the truth are not without some introduction to Moses, Isaiah and Jeremiah, and the rest of the prophets' (*Embassy for the Christians* 9).

So well were the prophets known that Athenagoras does not think it ridiculous to assume that even the Roman Emperors were acquainted with them. And of this same Athengoras, Philip of Side tells us that he planned to write an attack on the Christians. In order to do so he read the Holy Scriptures, and at the end of the reading the would-be attacker had become the defender of the faith.

The books of the Old Testament were accepted as Holy Scripture because in them men found God and God found men. Through all the centuries that continued to happen, and it can still happen today. Men can never afford to discard the books in which God speaks.

Part II

The Making of the New Testament

THE MOST SURPRISING thing about the making of the New Testament is the length of time which it required. The first time that we meet a list of New Testament books exactly the same as our list today, is in the Thirty-ninth Easter Letter of Athanasius which was written in AD 367. That is to say, it took more than three hundred years for the New Testament to reach its final form.

From the very beginning it could be said that Christianity was the religion of a book. It was in Judaism that Christianity was cradled; all the first Christians were Jews; and it was, therefore, natural and inevitable that the Christian service should follow the pattern of the service in the Jewish Synagogue.

The Synagogue service fell into three sections. The first section was a service of prayer and worship; the second was the reading of Scripture; the third consisted of teaching and explanation of the Law. It was for the second section that the whole service existed; it was in the reading of the Law that the whole service reached its centre and its peak. It was that service which the Christian Church took over.

Even in the New Testament itself there are signs that the reading of Scripture was very much in the forefront. In the Pastoral Epistles the message is sent to the Church: 'Till I come, give attention to *reading*, to exhortation, to teaching' (1 Timothy 4:13). In the Revelation the promise is: 'Blessed is he who *reads*, and they who hear the words of this prophecy' (Revelation 1:3), and the reference is not to private but to public reading. There are plain indications that, at least within the congregations to which they were addressed, the letters of Paul were to be read in public. 'I charge you,' he writes to the Thessalonians, 'that this letter be read to all the holy brethren' (1 Thessalonians 5:27). He writes to the Colossians: 'When this letter is read among you, cause that it be read also in the Church of the Laodiceans; and that you likewise read the letter from Laodicea' (Colossians 4:16).

In the First Apology of Justin Martyr there is the first description of a Christian service:

> 'On the day called the Day of the Sun all who live in cities or in the country gather together to one place, and the memoirs of the apostles or the writings of the prophets are read, as long as time permits; then, when the reader has ceased, the president verbally instructs, and exhorts to the imitation of these good things. Then we all rise together and pray.'
>
> (Justin Martyr, *First Apology* 67)

Right in the centre of the service is the reading of the word.

But for long the Christian Church had no literature of its own, and the book which was read was the Old Testament, for, when the Church began, there was no such thing as a book called the New Testament or any part of it: the books of the New Testament still had to be written. And here we come upon another surprise. Clearly the centre of the Christian message is the life and death of Jesus, and the extraordinary thing is the long delay before the Gospels were written. Mark is the earliest of the Gospels, and Mark cannot be dated before AD 60; Matthew and Luke were written between AD 80 and 90; and John dates to about AD 100. That is to say, the first Gospel which we possess was not written until about thirty years after the death of Jesus. Here, then, is the first problem which we must solve. Why was there this long delay in the production of a specifically Christian literature? It seems that many reasons combined to bring about that delay.

The Old Testament—A Christian Book

(1) For long the Church was content with the Old Testament; the Old Testament had become a Christian book. Had not everything that the Old Testament hoped for and foretold come true in Jesus? Had not the great promised Messianic age dawned in him? This was made all the easier because the first Christians were Jews and were, therefore, trained in the technique of the interpretation of Scripture for special purposes.

It was a Jewish belief that all Scripture had four meanings—*Peshat*, which was the simple meaning which could be seen at the first reading; *Remaz*, which was the suggested meaning and the truth which the passage suggested to the seeking mind; *Derush*, which was the meaning when all the resources of investigation, linguistic, historical, literary, archaeological, had been brought to bear upon the passage; and *Sod,* which was the inner and allegorical meaning. The initial letters of these words, P R D S, are the consonants of the word PaRaDiSe, and to enter into these three meanings was as if to enter into the bliss of Paradise. Now of all the meanings, *Sod*, the inner, mystical meaning, was the most important. The Jews were, therefore, skilled in finding inner meanings in Scripture. It was thus not difficult for them to develop a technique of Old Testament interpretation which discovered Jesus Christ all over the Old Testament.

38

We take an instance from the Letter of Barnabas (9:7, 8). It is argued therein that when Abraham circumcised his household (Genesis 17:23, 27), he did so looking forward in the Spirit to Jesus Christ. The number circumcised was 318. In Greek there are no signs for the numerals, and the letters of the alphabet are used as numerals as well as letters. So a=1 and b=2, and so on. Let us then take this number. 318 is denoted by the two letters *iota* and *eta*, which are the first two letters of the name *Jesus*, and, therefore, the number 18 stands for Jesus; 300 is denoted by the letter *tau*, which is the shape of the Cross, and therefore the number 300 stands for the Cross. Thus in the number 318 is discovered a message of Jesus and his Cross. When the Old Testament was consistently treated like this, it was not difficult to use it as a Christian book which everywhere spoke of and foretold Jesus Christ. Therefore it is not surprising that for some considerable time the early Church found the Old Testament enough.

(2) In Palestine the early Church came into a non-literary situation, and there were at least three reasons why the Church was unlikely to produce books:

(a) It was a long time before the days when printing had been invented. Book production was slow and laborious and distribution was very limited. Even when books were produced and copied by hand, it was an expensive process. A book consisted of papyrus sheets joined horizontally to form a roll. Papyrus cost between fourpence and a shilling (in pre-decimal money) for a sheet ten inches by eight. That is why poorer people often used *ostraca*, broken pieces of pottery, and the back of papyrus sheets which had already been used, for their writing.

Copying was by no means a cheap process. For the purposes of copying, a manuscript was divided into *stichoi*. The Greek word *stichos* means *a line*. In poetry the line is an obvious unit of measurement, but in prose an artificial unit had to be adopted. So the *stichos* for the purpose of copying was reckoned at the average length of a Homeric hexameter line, which is fifteen or sixteen syllables. In manuscripts the number of *stichoi* is often given at the end. In one manuscript Matthew has 2480 *stichoi*; Mark 1543; Luke 2714; John 1950; Acts 2610; 3 John 31: Revelation 1292. The Edict of Diocletian issued in the middle of the third century fixed the prices of most things, and it fixed the price of copying at 20-25 *denarii* per 100 *stichoi*. A denarius was worth about ninepence, so that it cost not far short of a pound to copy 100 *stichoi*. On this basis a professional copyist would charge about £50 or $150 to copy from Luke to Acts alone. It is quite clear that for ordinary people books at that price were out of the question.

(b) Especially in Palestine the normal way of transmitting knowledge was by oral transmission. The Rabbis had in fact a dislike of writing. 'Commit nothing to writing,' they said. For centuries they passed down the Oral Law by word of mouth, and a good student had to have a good memory so that he would be like 'a well plastered cistern' which never loses a drop. It was not until sometime in the third century that the Oral Law was written down. It was called the *Mishnah* and in English translation it makes a book of about 800 pages, and all of it had for centuries been orally transmitted. Papias, who was a great collector of information in the early Church, says that he questioned everyone he could find who had come into contact with Jesus and with the Apostles and their companions, 'for,' he says, 'I did not think that what was to be gotten from books would profit me as much as what came from the living and abiding voice' (Eusebius, *The Ecclesiastical History* 3.39.4). The Church grew up in a situation in which it was more natural to transmit knowledge orally than to commit to writing.

(c) The great majority of the early Christians did not, in fact, come from educated circles. Not many wise men after the flesh, not many mighty, not many noble were called (1 Corinthians 1:26). When Celsus attacked Christianity in the early part of the third century, he said that the attitude of the Christians was: 'Let no cultured person draw near, none wise, none sensible, for all that kind of thing we count evil; but, if any man is ignorant, if any man is wanting in sense and culture, if any man is a fool, let him boldly come'. As Celsus saw the Church, it was 'the simpletons, the ignoble, the senseless, slaves, womanfolk and children' whom Celsus wished to persuade (Origen, *Against Celsus* 3.44). Celsus, of course, was attacking Christianity as a hostile critic, but it was true that the Christian community was the last kind of community to be likely to produce literary works.

The situation of the early Church was a non-literary situation in which books in any case would not be readily or easily produced.

Apostles—The Living Books

(3)   So long as the original Apostles survived there was no need for written records of the life and words of Jesus. The Apostles were the eye-witnesses who knew. They were at once the repositories and the guarantors of Christian truth. They were the living books on which Jesus had written his message. Further, as Floyd V Filson points out, the recitation of the facts of Jesus' life, and the words of Jesus' teaching, was not enough; the events of Jesus' life and the substance of his teaching needed more than transmission, they needed also *interpretation*, and it was that authoritative interpretation that the Apostles alone could supply.

There is another side to this. The first age of the Church

was far more an age of the Spirit than an age of books. As Filson puts it: 'God was writing the gospel on the hearts of the converts to the faith'. The message was being demonstrated and passed on far more by persons than by pages in a book.

(4) One of the things which was most influential in delaying the production of a Christian literature was the Christian belief in the imminence of the Second Coming. The Christians expected the return of Jesus at any moment. In 1 Corinthians Paul recommends against marriage, because the Christians, as he at that time thought, were living in a situation in which it was unwise to enter into any ties or obligations. 'The time is short . . . The fashion of the world is passing away' (1 Corinthians 7:29, 31). The whole belief in these early days was that men were living in a quite impermanent situation, which might last only a few days or even a few hours, and in a situation like that books were an irrelevancy. There was no point in recording things for a posterity who would never be there to read the records. The belief in the immediacy of the Second Coming produced a situation in which books could not be regarded as anything else but unnecessary.

Such were the main circumstances in the situation which prevented and delayed the production of a Christian literature, but as time went on the production of that literature became a necessity.

End of the Oral Tradition .

(1) The time of oral tradition was bound to end with the death of the Apostles, and with the exception of John all the Apostles were dead by AD 70. Something had to be found to take the place of 'the living and abiding voice', and that something could not be anything other than a written record. There are many descriptions and accounts

of the writing of the Gospels in the works of the fathers, and again and again the implication is that the written Gospel was a substitute for the living apostle. Eusebius in his account of the writing of the Gospels (*The Ecclesiastical History* 3.24.5) tells us that Matthew preached to the Hebrews, and when he was about to leave them to go and preach to others, he committed his Gospel to writing, and thus 'compensated by his writing for the loss of his presence'.

It is the consistent tradition of the early Church that Mark was 'the interpreter' of Peter and that his Gospel is nothing other than the preaching material which Peter used, and that Luke's Gospel is really the gospel which Paul preached. Irenaeus (*Against Heresies* 3.1.1,2) speaks about the preaching of Peter and Paul and of their foundation of the Roman Church. He goes on to say: 'After their death, Mark, the disciple and interpreter of Peter, handed down to us in writing the things preached by Peter. Luke also, the follower of Paul, put down in a book the gospel preached by that one'. The clear implication is that the written Gospel was an attempt to compensate for the death of the great preachers. The Monarchian Prologue to the Forth Gospel says that John wrote 'when he realized that the day of his departure had come', and Jerome says that he finished his Gospel 'with fortunate haste' before death overtook him (Jerome, *The Prologues to the Four Gospels*).

The written Gospels were meant to compensate for the loss of the living voice of the Apostles.

(2) When Christianity left the narrower bounds of Palestine and went into the Greek-Roman world, it entered a world where books were familiar things and where publishing and bookselling were part of big business. Atticus, Cicero's friend and publisher, was the first man to reproduce books in a big way. The bookshops of Rome were covered

with advertisements for new books, and became the literary *salons* of their day. Books were multiplied by being dictated to fifty or even a hundred slave scribes at the one time; and this made for speed in copying, even if it did produce books in which mistakes were all too frequent. In this way a book like Martial's epigrams could be copied in about seventeen hours, and an edition of a thousand copies could easily be produced in a month.

Bookselling and book distribution were also highly organized and books penetrated everywhere. Varro wrote a series of seven hundred short biographies, and Pliny said that he had succeeded in conferring omnipresence on the people of whom he wrote. *The Life of Martin of Tours* by Sulpicius Severus was a bestseller. A friend of the author found people reading it in Carthage; he went on to Alexandria and found people reading it there; everywhere he went in Egypt he found the book; and even came upon an old man reading it in the middle of the desert. Further, books thus copied and distributed were naturally not nearly so expensive. The first book of Martial has 119 epigrams comprising some 700 lines, and it could be produced and sold for five denarii, which is about four shillings.

When Christianity went out to a literary world like this, it too began to see the immense value of the written word; and it is not without significance that Mark, the first Gospel, was almost certainly written and issued in Rome.

(3) The written word was of immense value for the missionary work of the Church. In the very earliest days the class of Church officials called the *teachers* (1 Corinthians 12:8) must have been of primary importance. They must have been the people trained and instructed in the facts of the Gospel story and in the basic doctrines of the faith, and it is to them that new converts must have been handed over for instruction in the faith. But when

44

Christianity was sweeping across Asia Minor and Europe, it is clear that the travelling missionaries and evangelists could not spend very long in one place, and it must have been of immense value to them to have a written account of the life and teaching of Jesus, which they could leave with their converts when they were compelled to move on. To this day it is one of the first tasks of the missionary to learn the language of the people amongst whom he or she works, and then to translate the Gospel story into that language, even if it means, as it often does, that an alphabet has to be invented and a grammar and syntax created. It is easy to see that in its missionary work the Church has no greater instrument and weapon than a written account of the Gospel which it seeks to sow among men.

(4) As the years went on, men began to see that the Second Coming was not going to be so immediate as once they had expected it to be. That is to say, they began to see that they were living in a more or less permanent situation. This would completely change their attitude to the written word. Books, which had once seemed to be irrelevant, became of the greatest importance for the teaching of the facts of the Gospel story, and the setting out and the explanation of Christian belief and the Christian ethic. As the hope of the Second Coming receded more and more into the distant future, the written book became more and more important in the life and work of the Church.

(5) As time went on, the Church began to need a prophylactic against heresy. A vital Church will always be a Church liable to produce heresies and deviations. There will never be any heresy when men do not think for themselves, and when they do think for themselves there will always be the danger that they will venture down the wrong pathways. So in the early Church there were those

who misunderstood, and those who twisted and distorted the Gospel. Many of them claimed that they had their own private revelations and their own private Gospels. Jerome, thinking of the preface to Luke's Gospel, says that Luke wrote 'to correct those who had written with too much haste'. He speaks of those who had 'attempted without the Spirit and grace of God to draw up a story rather than to defend the truth of history'. He compares them to the false prophets who followed their own spirits rather than the Spirit of God. Clearly the Church needed a touchstone of orthodoxy against which false Gospels, distorted theologies, and unethical ethics could be judged; and for that purpose nothing could be so efficacious as an official written Gospel. The rise of heresies made an orthodox account of the facts and the faith of Christianity nothing short of an essential.

The Need for a Written Literature

(6) The Church needed a written literature for apologetic purposes.

(a) It needed a written literature for apologetic purposes in regard to the Jews. We have only to read Acts to see that the Church is founded on the Resurrection. The Church was the Resurrection community; the Resurrection was 'the star in the firmament of Christianity'. An account of the Resurrection would, therefore, be needed. But the Resurrection was preceded by the Cross, and the story of the Cross would need to be told.

Here is the fact which explains the 'shape' of the Gospels. Any careful reader must be struck by the apparently disproportionate place the last days of Jesus' life occupy in the Gospels. It is only in the last week that we can anything like follow Jesus day to day. Eight out of Matthew's twenty-eight chapters, six out of Mark's sixteen, eight out of Luke's twenty-four, are taken up with the story of the last days; and in John, Jesus arrives in Jerusalem in chapter 10 and never seems to leave it again. The explanation for this is that the Gospels, as it were, were written and built up backwards. It was from the Resurrection and the Cross that the story began, and the rest was introduction to that. The supreme events were set down first and set down at length.

Now here, in regard to the Jews, there was an acute problem. For the Jews a crucified Messiah was a complete impossibility, for cursed was every man who hung upon a tree (Deuteronomy 21:23; Galatians 3:13). There was only one argument which could convince the Jews, and that was to take the life and the death of Jesus and to show that every part and action of it was in fact a fulfilment of prophecy, and that all this had long since been foretold. To do this there was needed an account of the outstanding events in Jesus' life, and a record of the prophecies of which they were claimed to be the fulfilments. It may well be that before there ever was a consecutive Gospel there was a book of Testimonies which did exactly that. And this is the explanation of the ever-recurring phrase in Matthew that this and that event happened so that the saying of the prophet might be fulfilled.

To convince the Jews that Jesus was the Messiah, although he had been crucified, it was necessary to have an account of his life in which it was shown that from beginning to end it was the fulfilment of prophecy; hence a written Gospel became imperative for apologetic to the Jews.

(b) When persecution arose, as Jesus said that it would arise, a written account of the life of Jesus was necessary for two reasons. First, it was necessary to have an account of the life and teaching of Jesus to show to the Roman government in order to convince the Romans that

Jesus was a good man, and that Christianity was a sound and useful influence, and to convince them that Jesus was not a criminal and that the Christians were not revolutionaries. The written Gospel became a necessity so that it might be used as a brief in the defence of the Christian faith when it was attacked by the state. Second, such an account was necessary for the sake of those who were persecuted. If they could be helped to see that what had come upon them was something of which Jesus had given warning and which he had foretold, and if they could be enabled to see that in their agony Jesus was with them, and that he never called on any man to suffer that which he himself had not suffered, then the Christians had a great help and support when life became an agonizing thing. The written Gospel was a precious help in time of trouble in the days when the Church was under fire.

(c) When the Christian preachers went out into the world, it would be of the greatest help to them to have an account of Christianity which they could put into the hands of intelligent, thinking people who were interested in this new faith. This is, for instance, what the Prologue to the Fourth Gospel seeks to do. It seeks to express Christianity in language and in categories of thought which the educated Greek could grasp and understand, and with which he was familiar. The Gospel became an apologetic weapon with which to appeal to the thinkers among the Romans and the Greeks. It made the Christian faith something which was not altogether dependent on the voice of a preacher, but which they could ponder and study in their own homes, and in their own groups, and at their leisure.

(7) A written Gospel was of the greatest use for ecclesiastical purposes. The Church was bound to have its problems; the leaders of the Church were bound to have to come to their decisions; the local Churches would

inevitably arrive in situations which were puzzling and difficult. On such occasions it was of incalculable help to have a book in which some relevant word or command of Jesus could readily be found. The written Gospels provided the Church with a law by which all problems could be illuminated and by which all actions and all situations could be judged.

It is true that the circumstances of the early Church long delayed the production of a written Christian literature, but it is also true that the day came when the circumstances of the Church rendered the production of such a literature nothing less than completely essential.

The Words of Jesus

There are still two more particular reasons why a written Christian literature was bound to emerge.

First, there was the supreme reverence for the words of Jesus. The Church emerged from a Jewish society which was accustomed to handing down the most precious teaching by word of mouth; but once the Church had gone out into the larger world, the time was bound to come when the words of Jesus would be written down, lest anything of these words of life should be lost. To commit a thing to writing is the most certain way to its fixed preservation, and, for that, if for no other reason the words of Jesus were bound to be written down.

Second, there was the basic idea of a covenant. A covenant is a relationship between God and man, entered into on the sole initiative of the grace and love of God. But that covenant has its conditions; obedience to the law of God is essential, if it is to be maintained. The covenant, therefore, needs its book of the law (Exodus 24:7). The older covenant, the covenant between God and the people of Israel, had its book. But Christ was the end of the law

49

(Romans 10:4). The law came by Moses, but grace and truth came by Jesus Christ (John 1:17). As Harnack states it, if the handwriting that was against us was blotted out (Colossians 2:14), the handwriting that is for us had to be written down. Hence the new covenant needed its book, just as the old covenant had its book. The idea of a covenant brings along with it the necessity of a book of the covenant, and the New Testament *is* that book.

At this stage a necessary, and extremely important, question arises. There was this lengthy delay in the production of a written Christian literature. Mark, the earliest Gospel, dates to not earlier than AD 60. What was happening to the story in the time in between? Was it being in any way falsified, elaborated, distorted? In view of the thirty-year delay, can we trust the story in the Gospels? Can we accept it as accurate and dependable, or must we admit that things could have happened to it in the thirty years which made it in its written form less than accurate? We may be quite sure that the Gospel narrative as we have it is a reliable and trustworthy account of the life and words of Jesus for three reasons:

(1) There is a wide difference between the quality of the ancient and the modern memory. It is true that the printed book has ruined the human memory. It is now for the most part not necessary to carry a thing in the memory, for at any time a book may be consulted, and the necessary information obtained; but in the ancient world it was largely true that, if a man wished to possess a thing, he had to remember it.

Xenophon (*Symposium* 3.6) tells us of a cultured Greek called Niceratus. Antisthenes asks Niceratus in what knowledge he takes pride, and Niceratus answers: 'My father was anxious to see me develop into a good man, and as a means to this end he compelled me to memorize all Homer; and so even now I can repeat the whole *Iliad* and *Odyssey* by heart'. The *Iliad* and the *Odyssey* each contains twenty-four books, and each book contains at least five hundred lines, and yet for a Greek this was not an uncommon feat of memory. In commenting on this passage, T R Glover points out that in Finland there are people who had to learn the whole of the *Kalevala*, the national epic, at school by heart—twenty thousand lines in three years. Nonetheless, the retentiveness of the ancient memory was much greater than the modern memory; and in the ancient world there was much less chance of material being either forgotten or distorted.

(2) It must never be forgotten that all the stories of Jesus' life and all the material of Jesus' teaching were constant preaching material. The repeating of it was not dependent on one man's memory; the memory was a communal memory. The stories were continually being repeated and were constantly being used, and any deviation from them would quite inevitably be noticed and pounced upon. For the material of the life and teaching of Jesus, we are not dependent on single individuals; we are dependent on the memory of the Church.

(3) We may put this in another way. The stories about Jesus and the teaching of Jesus became stereotyped very early on. Anyone who has to do with children knows that a favourite story has always to be told in the same way, and any deviation from the known and loved form of the story is at once noted, and correction and retelling are at once demanded. It was thus that the form of the gospel material was very early fixed and finalized.

The 'Forms' of the Gospel

The realization of this has produced a recent development in New Testament scholarship. It has produced the science of what is called Form Criticism. The basic contention of this science is that the Gospels are composed of units of teaching material, and that these units fall into certain fixed and unvarying forms. Five of these forms have been identified and distinguished.

(1) There are *Paradigms, Apothegms*, or *Pronouncement* Stories. These are stories which are preserved solely for the sake of some notable saying which they contain and to which they lead up. The importance lies entirely in the saying, and the events of the incident simply form a setting for the jewel of the saying. For instance, the story of the plucking of the ears of corn on the Sabbath day exists solely to enshrine the saying, 'The Sabbath was made for man, and not man for the Sabbath' (Mark 2:23-28). The story of the call of Matthew exists solely to preserve the saying, 'I came not to call the righteous but sinners to repentance (Matthew 9:9-13). The story of the tribute money exists to hand down the saying, 'Render to Caesar the things that are Caesar's, and to God the things that are God's' (Mark 12:13-17). All over the Gospels there are these units of teaching which exist to preserve some important saying of Jesus.

(2) There are *Tales* or *Novellen*. These are stories which depict Jesus exercising a wonderful and miraculous power over nature and over human nature. They exist, not to enshrine some saying, but to retain the memory of some significant event. They almost always follow the same pattern. They give a history of the illness, an account of the cure, and the result of the cure. Such a story is the story of the healing of the lame man at the pool (John 5:1-9); the opening of the eyes of the man born blind (John 9:1-7); the stilling of the storm (Mark 4:35-41); the feeding of the five thousand (Mark 6:32-44). These stories exist to preserve the story, not of something which Jesus said, but of something which Jesus did.

(3) There are *Sayings*. These are sayings of Jesus

52

which are preserved in isolation, without a context. They are collections of the sayings of Jesus made for teaching purposes. The best example of such a collection of sayings is the Sermon on the Mount. In this case the saying is so epigrammatic and so intrinsically memorable that it needs no context and no story as its setting, and it is preserved by itself or in conjunction with other connected sayings.

The two final groups of sayings are described by two words used in a technical sense, and it is to be noted that the use of these words does not necessarily prejudge the historicity of the incidents which they are used to describe:

(4) There are *Legends*. These are stories written for edification about extraordinary happenings involving a holy man or a holy place. The best examples of these stories are the Birth and Infancy stories of Jesus. In these stories there is always the element of the extraordinary, and there is always an extraordinary person involved.

(5) There are *Myths*. The Greek used the word *muthos*, myth, in a quite technical sense. He used it of a story which is an attempt 'to state the eternal, the spiritual, and the divine in the language and pictures of time, matter and humanity'. Myths are stories which are attempts to state in human language and human pictures that which is essentially beyond human language to state at all. Such stories are the stories of the Baptism, the Transfiguration, and the Temptations.

Into these forms the stories about Jesus and the record of his teaching became stereotyped. They were all used for preaching and for instruction and for missionary purposes. In all cases there was a *point* to be made and presented in the most vivid and memorable and cogent way possible; and, therefore, it was entirely natural that such stories would become fixed and stereotyped and unalterable in form. Just because of this we can be certain that in the years between, the gospel story and the teaching of Jesus did not suffer distortion or elaboration but were handed down in unvarying form.

'This has the most important consequences. It means that the Gospels are in fact the possession of the Church; it means that they embody a social tradition, which was the common property of all the Churches, and which did not rest on the recollections of a few individuals. The significance of this is obvious. The memories of a few individuals might be mistaken—since human recollection is notoriously fallible—but the testimony of a group, even if anonymous, is more likely to have been verified, criticized, supported, culled, and selected during the first generation of early Church evangelism. The possibility of fabrication by one or two individuals is completely ruled out.'

(F C Grant, *The Gospels*)

The thirty years of apparent silence need trouble no one; the circumstances in which the material of the Gospels was handed down are the best guarantee of its reliability.

How the New Testament Emerged

How then did the Canon of the New Testament emerge, and how was it built up?

Once a Christian literature began to be written it flourished almost luxuriantly. Luke tells us that many before him had taken it upon themselves to give an account of the Gospel events (Luke 1:1). Jerome, in his Prologues to the Four Gospels, tells us of many Gospels: the Gospel according to the Egyptians, the Gospels according to Thomas and Matthias and Bartholomew, the Gospels of the Twelve Apostles, and of Basilides, and Apelles, and of the rest. It would take too long, he says, to enumerate them all, and many, if not all, were dangerous and heretical. Equally, many books of Acts had emerged: the Acts of Thomas and Andrew and Philip and Peter and John, the Acts of Paul and Thecla. There were other Apocalypses beside the one Apocalypse of John which gained a place in the New Testament, such as the Apocalypse of Peter.

There were many books which in certain Churches were at least for a time accepted as Scripture, although they were never accepted by the whole Church. Such books were *The Teaching of the Twelve Apostles, The First Letter of Clement to Rome, The Letter of Barnabas, The Shepherd of Hermas.* What in this mass of literature was to be regarded as Scripture, and what was not? What was to be completely banished and discarded, what was to be tolerated, and even encouraged, for private reading? And what was to become part of the actual Canon of the New Testament?

There was one thing which gave a book prestige and authority, and which set it well on the way to being fully regarded as Scripture; that was, its reading at the public worship of the Church. Once a book began to be so read, it had acquired a status which lifted it out of the ruck of ordinary literature. For a book to be read at the public worship of the Church and for a book to be canonical, came to very nearly the same thing. So, then, its being read at public worship was the first thing to single out a book.

But who was it who took the decision that a book should be so used, or who decided that a book must not be so used, or that its usage in such a way must cease?

The early Church was characteristically a Church of the Spirit, and this, as Harnack points out, had in two ways much to do with this process of selection.

First, there were men who were men of the Spirit *par*

excellence. These were the prophets, the Apostles, and the teachers. When they gave a decision, that decision had to be obeyed. They were the watchdogs and the sentinels and the guardians of the faith. They would be quick to see anything which would damage the faith, which would distort it, which would deflect the minds and thoughts of men from the true way. They could seal any document with their approval, and equally they could eject it with their disapproval. Beyond a doubt this is a right which such men did exercise. Augustine tells us that it was the decision of *sancti et docti homines,* holy and learned men, which prevented the documents of the Manichaens from being regarded as Scripture. It was such men who under the guidance of the Spirit decided what should be read, and what should not be read, at the services of the Church.

Second, when a congregation of the Christians was meeting as a community of Christ, and when it was conscious that it was so doing, it was always deeply conscious that it was meeting and acting and deciding under the influence of the Spirit. When Paul gave judgment regarding the disciplining of a certain man, he said, 'I have already pronounced judgment in the name of the Lord Jesus' (1 Corinthians 5:3, 4). Clement writing to the Corinthians dared to say: 'What we have said, God has said through us' (1 Clement 59). 'We have spoken or written through the Holy Spirit' (1 Clement 63). When the decisions of the Council of Jerusalem were announced, they were announced with the words: 'The Holy Spirit and we have decided (Acts 15:28). 'The Church in solemn assembly was especially an organ of the Spirit' (Harnack). The Church, therefore, could and did decide what books it would use in its own public worship, and what books it would mark with its disapproval, and the approval of any book was its first step on the road to its full and final acceptance as Holy Scripture.

A question of the first importance now arises. Assuming that men of the Spirit, and Christian assemblies acting under the Spirit, had a very great deal to do with sealing books with approval or rejecting them with disapproval, what was the standard which they used to assess the value of a book? By what yardstick was a book judged? The answer to that is clear and unmistakable. The test which was applied to every book was—Is it, or is it not, apostolic? Was it written by an apostle, or at least by a man who was in direct contact with the circle of the Apostles? Apostolicity and canonicity went hand in hand. There were reasons for this:

The Apostolic Authority

(1) The older any institution grows, the more it is likely to worship its past, especially if that past has been undeniably great and glorious. 'The more perplexing, troublous, and feeble the present appeared, the more sacred became its own past, the time of creative energy, with all that belonged thereto,' and 'tradition always means the need of the present appealing to the authority of the past' (Harnack). The Apostles appeared to be clad with a certain aura of forgotten and unsurpassable greatness simply because they belonged to what was looked back on as the great age of the Church.

(2) But there was more than a mere worship of the past, as, indeed, Harnack was careful to say. In the Church the Apostles held a place that no others could ever hold. It is quite true that very soon most of them vanished from history, and our knowledge of any of them is astonishingly meagre. But they were always looked on as the future rulers and judges of the Messianic kingdom, and they were always regarded as men who had been uniquely in the confidence of Jesus. Did not Jesus say: 'I appoint

57

unto you a kingdom, as my Father has appointed unto me' (Luke 22:29). 'He that receiveth you receiveth me (Matthew 10:40)? Could not Paul say to the Galatians: 'You received me as Christ Jesus' (Galatians 4:14)? Were not the twelve foundation stones of the holy city, the new Jerusalem, inscribed with the names of the twelve Apostles (Revelation 21:14)? Serapion, around AD 200, could say: 'We receive both Peter and the other Apostles as Christ'.

It was a standard idea held by the Jews that he who is sent is in some sense equal to him who sends. The delegate is equal to the person who sends him out as his representative on his task. So without irreverence, when they were thinking of the bringing of the Christian message and the Christian truth, they could say that Jesus equals God, and the Apostles equal Jesus. Clement of Rome writes:

> 'The Apostles were made evangelists to us by the Lord Christ: Jesus Christ was sent by God. Thus Christ is from God and the Apostles from Christ. He and they came into being from the will of God in harmony. The Church is built on them as a foundation.'
>
> (1 Clement 42)

The Apostles had a place, and a rightful place, as the supreme representatives of Jesus, and as the supreme bearers of his message and interpreters of his purposes. The Church was not wrong when it made apostolicity its acid test.

(3) But there was something perhaps even more important yet. Any historical religion comes to a time when attestation is of the first importance. Attestation, according to Harnack, can be as important as the revelation to which it attests. Christianity is founded on certain historical facts, on an entry of God into the

historical situation. And the supreme question is—*Are these facts true?* In the early Church, that was of the first importance. Many of the heretical sects, such as the Gnostics, claimed that he had private revelation. Basilides, for instance, claimed that he had received special information from Glaukias, who, so it was said, was an interpreter of Peter. Valentinus claimed that his version of Christianity came by way of Theodas who was, so it was said, a friend of Paul. Some claimed that their particular brand of teaching was based on a private revelation given by Jesus himself to a chosen few.

Apart altogether from the claims of the heretics within the Church, there is the fact that the pagan world was full of stories of dying and rising gods. There were such stories in every Mystery Religion. Pagan mythology is full of them. And the obvious question was—Is this Jesus only another of these dying and rising gods? Is he no more than the centre of another myth? Or, is he a real person, and did the things which are told about him really and truly happen?

Obviously only one thing can settle the question—unimpeachable and undeniable attestation going back to eye-witnesses of the facts. Now that is what the Apostles alone could give. 'We lay it down,' said Tertullian, 'that the evangelical instrument has the Apostles as its authors, upon whom this duty of promulgating the gospel was laid by the Lord Himself' (Tertullian, *Against Marcion* 4.2). The only real attestation was evidence brought and given by eye-witnesses to the facts, and that which the Apostles alone could supply. What the Church had to have was an unbroken human chain of reliable witness going back to the historical facts of the life, the death, and the Resurrection of Jesus Christ. What troubled John Bunyan in the days of his uncertainty was that the Jews thought *their* religion the best, and the Mohammedans thought *their* religion the best; and he was afraid that Christianity might be only a *think so* too. Without this unanswerable attestation Christianity was abundantly right in making the apostolic witness the foundation of her faith.

The test of any book was—Is it, or is it not, apostolic? —and it was a good and right test. The weight which was attached to this standard of apostolicity may be seen in Tertullian's account of the Gospels. Matthew and John pass the test of apostolicity without question. But what of the other two Gospels? Tertullian goes on to say: 'What Mark edited may be affirmed to be of Peter, whose interpreter Mark was: and as for Luke's account, men are accustomed to ascribe it to Paul'. Mark's and Luke's claims to acceptance come from their association with men who were Apostles.

We are now in a position to examine in detail the actual process of the building up of the New Testament. Before a book can become canonical it has to undergo certain stages of development. It has to be written; it has to be widely read; it has to be accepted as useful for life and for doctrine; it has to make its way into the public worship of the Church; it has to win acceptance not simply locally but throughout the whole Church; and finally it has to be officially approved by the voice and decision of the Church.

The First Christian Books

The first Christian books to form a collection were the letters of Paul. Even within the New Testament itself there is proof that they existed as a collection and that they were well known; for the writer of 2 Peter refers to them as if they were perfectly familiar to his readers, even if he does say that they have their difficult passages, and that certain heretical thinkers have twisted their teaching for their own ends (2 Peter 3:16). Clement of Rome, writing to the Church at Corinth, could say: 'Take up the letter of the blessed Apostle Paul' (1 Clement 46:1) in the certainty that his readers possessed it, and that they were prepared to grant it respect at least, if not authority. Ignatius can write to the Ephesians reminding them that Paul remembers them in every letter (Ignatius, Ephesians 12:2). Polycarp, writing to the Philippians, reminds his readers that Paul in his absence wrote letters to them by the study of which they can build themselves up in the faith which had been given to them (Polycarp, Philippians 3:2). It is clear that by AD 100 Paul's letters had been collected and were widely known and widely accepted.

There is a sense in which this is very surprising. In almost every case Paul was writing to deal with a local and a temporary situation. Dark and dangerous heresies reared their heads, or threatened to arise; practical problems arose; troubles threatened the peace of some Church; and thereupon Paul, not being able to be everywhere personally present, sat down to write a letter to combat the mistaken thinkers, to give guidance for the practical problem, to seek to preserve the peace and unity of the Church.

Paul's letters were far from being theological treatises composed in the peace of a study or a library. They were meant to deal with an immediate situation in a definite community at a particular time.

'Paul had no thought of adding a few fresh compositions to the existing Jewish epistles, still less of enriching the sacred literature of his nation . . . He had no presentiment of the place his words would occupy in universal history, not so much that they would be in existence in the next generation, far less that one day people would look on them as Holy Scripture.'

(*Deissmann*)

At the same time, even when we have said that, it must still be remembered that there is no reason why something produced for an immediate situation should not become a universal possession cherished for all time. Every perfect love poem and love song, such as those of Robert Burns, was written for one person and has yet become a universal possession. The music of Bach was often written for Sunday by Sunday performance by his choir in Leipzig and is yet such that it will be performed so long as men everywhere know what music is. There is nothing unusual in a thing being temporary and local and immediate and yet at the same time having in it the seeds of a universal immortality.

It must be remembered that there are times when Paul goes out of his way to remind his readers that he is speaking as no more than a man. 'I speak in a human way,' he writes to the Romans (Romans 3:5). 'Concerning the unmarried,' he writes to the Corinthians, 'I have no command of the Lord, but I give my opinion as one who by the Lord's mercy is trustworthy' (1 Corinthians 7:25). 'What I am saying,' he says, 'I say not with the Lord's authority but as a fool, in this boastful confidence' (2 Corinthians 11:17). There were times when Paul made no claim to infallibility and made no claim that the divine voice spoke through him.

Still further, it is an astonishing fact that if we possessed only the Book of Acts, we would never have known that Paul had ever written a letter. Luke was the hero-worshipper of Paul, and from chapter 13 Acts becomes to all intents and purposes the biography of Paul, and yet Luke has nothing to say about Paul the letter writer. Sometimes Paul was by no means sure that his letters would be read by everyone. 'I adjure you,' he writes to the Thessalonians, 'by the Lord that this letter be read to all the brethren' (1 Thessalonians 5:27). So little attention was paid to his letters, that we know that many, and in particular a letter which had to do with Laodicea (Colossians 4:16) were lost and vanished from sight.

Collecting Paul's Letters

In view of all this, how were Paul's letters collected, and how did they become the universal possession of the Church? There were, of course, ample precedents for the collection and publication of the letters of great men. The letters of Plato and Cicero had been collected and published. How did Paul's letters attain to the dignity of collection and publication, and how did they in the end gain their place of authority as Holy Scripture? At the moment we shall try to answer only the first half of that question, and the answer to the second half will come later. We have certain pointers to aid us in our investigation.

It is significant that in writings before AD 90 there is no mention of the letters of Paul and no reference to them. In writings after AD 90 there are abundant references to the letters of Paul and abundant proof of full acquaintance with them. In the Synoptic Gospels, even in Luke, there is no trace of Pauline language or ideas. But in the Fourth Gospel, in James, in 2 Peter, and in the Letters of John there is clear acquaintance with Pauline thought and language. Obviously something must have happened to bring this about.

Further, it is significant that from AD 90 onwards there came into the Church what E J Goodspeed calls 'a shower of Christian letters'. Consider the beginning of the Revelation. The Revelation begins with the letters to the Seven Churches. Why should a book begin with a collection of letters? Why should Pergamum read the letter to Ephesus, and Thyatira read the letter to Laodicea, and Philadelphia read the letter to Smyrna? The very way in which the Revelation begins shows that there must have been a precedent for issuing a collection of letters. It may well have been close to that time that Hebrews and James and Jude were written, as well as the letters of John, and most of these are not so much real letters as treatises cast in epistolary form. There must have been a good precedent for letter writing. It is certainly just shortly after this that Clement wrote his letter to Corinth. And it was not very long after this that Polycarp collected and issued the seven letters of Ignatius. Not long after AD 90 there was a veritable epidemic of letter writing and something must have given it impetus.

The deduction must be that it was just then that the letters of Paul were first collected and issued, and that this collection provided the precedent and the stimulus for this outbreak of letter writing.

But how did this happen? It was for long believed that the growth of the collection of Paul's letters was a long, slow process, a kind of natural growth. The idea was that a Church possessed a letter of Paul of its own; it knew that a neighbouring Church also had a letter; it asked for a copy of its neighbour's letter; and so bit by bit the collect-ion was built up, varying from place to place according to the number of letters each individual Church had been able to obtain, and coming to its completion somewhere towards the end of the century.

But more recently, E J Goodspeed and John Knox in America, and C L Mitton in Britain, have produced a quite different, and perhaps better, theory. We have to explain why, between AD 60 and AD 90, there is no trace of the letters of Paul. The above scholars think that the letters of Paul were forgotten, that they were seldom or never used; but laid away in some chest among the archives of their Churches, covered in dust, buried in neglect; that there was in fact a generation who did not know Paul.

What changed all that? We have seen that the change must have come not very long before AD 90. What happened to affect the situation somewhere between AD 80 and AD 90? The answer is that it was sometime near the middle of that decade that Acts was written and published, in its first form at least. The result was that the half-forgotten figure of Paul suddenly burst upon the Church as the most epic, the most heroic, the most colossal and dominating figure in the early history of the Church. Immediately everything about this extraordinary man became precious. Every relic of him must be rescued from oblivion; everything he wrote must be recovered and studied and revered. The publication of Acts suddenly reminded men of the half-forgotten greatness of the incomparable apostle to the Gentiles, and it was that which provided the stimulus to the collection and the publication of the letters of Paul.

Making the Collection

Can we go on to say where the collection was made and issued? There are certain indications which point strongly to Ephesus. It was there that Paul spent three years, longer than in any other place in the days of his freedom. It was there that Revelation with its seven letters was published; it was there that the Johannine letters with their knowledge of Paul were published; it was in Asia Minor that the Ignatian collection was made; and it is there that references to the letters of Paul as a collection appear. Ephesus was in any event what Harnack called 'the second fulcrum of Christianity', Antioch being the first. Goodspeed and Mitton both regard Ephesians as a letter produced by a disciple of Paul, who was soaked in the Pauline letters and especially in Colossians, as a preface and introduction to that collection. That may or may not be so; it is doubtful;

65

but it is in any event not an essential part of the theory. There is good evidence to suggest that it was in Ephesus, about AD 90, consequent upon the publication of Acts, that the Pauline letters were collected and published.

One last question arises—Can we say who was the moving figure behind this collection? Once again Goodspeed and Knox have a suggestion to make. True, we are now in the realm of conjecture, if not of imaginative reconstruction, but it is a suggestion of such interest and charm that it is more than worth while to look at it.

There is one letter in Paul's collection which stands out as different from all the others—and that is the letter to Philemon. It is a little personal note, quite different from the others. As long ago as Jerome, there were those who were saying that it was so trivial that it was quite out of place. It is certainly true that anyone must wonder how it succeeded in gaining an entry into the New Testament at all, and why it was included in the collection. For its inclusion there must be a reason. John Knox writes:

'The more anomalous the presence of Philemon in the collection appears, the more significant it must be. The more grounds which can be cited for its exclusion, the more important must have been the ground upon which it was actually included. The very fact that Philemon seems so out of place is evidence that the original editors had very good reason for including it. We are convinced that if we knew that reason we should know something very important about the publication of the Pauline letters.'

Can we then discover the reason for the inclusion of this little letter, so different from the others?

The letter is a letter about the sending back to Philemon of the runaway slave Onesimus. Onesimus must have become very dear to Paul. His name means 'the useful one' and Paul puns on that name. 'Formerly he was *useless* to you, but now indeed he is *useful* to you and to me' (v 11). Now let us hear what Paul says:

'I would have been glad to keep him with me, in order that he might serve me on your behalf during my imprisonment for the gospel, but I preferred to do nothing without your consent in order that your goodness might not be by compulsion but of your own free will.'

(Philemon, vv 13, 14)

Could there be a clearer indication that Paul would very much like to have Onesimus back again? And could the heart of Philemon have been proof against that gentle and courteous and half-humorous appeal?

Let us, then, assume that Paul received Onesimus back from Philemon as his personal helper and attendant. If that is so, Onesimus would become very much Paul's right-hand man.

And now let us go on more than fifty years hence, when, *if* Onesimus was still alive, he would be an old man. Ignatius is on his way to Rome to fight with the beasts in the arena. As he goes, he writes to the Church at Ephesus and he speaks of their bishop—'a man of indescribable charity and your bishop here on earth' (Ignatius, Ephesians 1:3). And what is the bishop's name? *It is Onesimus.* That is to say, at the very time when the Pauline collection was made at Ephesus, the name of the bishop was Onesimus. Can Onesimus the bishop be the same man as the run-away slave who had twined himself around the heart of Paul?

No man can say for certain, but it is possible. It may well be that, after the publication of Acts had drawn the full-length picture of Paul to the Church, and had given the stimulus to the collection and preservation of everything connected with this colossal figure, in Ephesus Onesimus took steps to collect and publish the letters of the master whom he had loved and who had loved him. And in that collection he included the little letter to Philemon, because it told of himself as a thieving and runaway slave. He left deliberately the record of his shame, as if to say: 'See what I was—and see what Jesus Christ did for me'. If that is so, it is one of the loveliest hidden romances of the New Testament, for it is a moving thing to think of the great and good bishop deliberately including the letter which told of what he once was, as if to say: 'That is what Christ did for me—and he can do it for you'.

In regard to Onesimus we are in the realm of conjecture, and all we can say is that we hope that this story may be true. But we may regard it as all but certain that the letters of Paul were collected in Ephesus in AD 90 as a consequence of the publication of Acts.

It is true that they are not yet fully Scripture—that final step is still to come—but C L Mitton was not wrong when he wrote: 'It may very well be that this acceptance of Paul's writings as authoritative was the first clear act in the formation of what later came to be the Canon of the New Testament'.

The Gospels Win their Place

We can now turn to the story of how the Gospels won their place as sacred Scripture.

Jesus himself wrote nothing and left no written book. It was not his writing but his *words* which were always quoted. 'Remember,' said Paul, 'the *words* of the Lord Jesus, how he said, It is more blessed to give than to receive' (Acts 20:35). 'Remember,' said Clement, 'the *words* of Jesus,

68

which he spoke, when he was teaching gentleness and long-suffering' (1 Clement 13:1). The Gospel began by being a spoken gospel, and for long it remained so. The Gospel, as Irenaeus says, was first proclaimed by the eye-witnesses of the saving events, and it was only afterwards that it was by the will of God handed down to us in the Scriptures to be the foundation and pillar of our faith (Irenaeus, *Against Heresies* 3. 1. 1).

In the early Church it is persons and not books who dominate the scene. It was not through books but through persons that the Gospel went out, and that the work of the Church was done. It was not a letter but Peter and John who were sent to Samaria by the Apostles, when the power of Christ began to work there (Acts 8:14). It was not a letter but Barnabas who was sent to Antioch when the great experiment of taking the Gospel to the Gentiles began there (Acts 11:22). Paul wrote letters, but again he used Timothy or Titus or Mark as well as the written word (1 Corinthians 4:17; 16:10,12; 2 Corinthians 7:6; 8:6; Philippians 2:19; Colossians 4:10; 1 Thessalonians 3:2).

The very words used of the spread of the Gospel are all speaking words. To receive the Gospel and its facts is *paralambanein*, and to pass it on to someone else is *paradidonai* (1 Corinthians 11:23; 15:3), and these are the Greek words which are characteristic of and special to oral tradition. The Gospel itself is *euaggelion—good news, glad tidings*—and only later came to mean a *kerussein,* which literally means *to proclaim as a herald.* The supreme function of the Christian is *marturia*, which is *personal witness.* The Gospel itself is *logos akoes,* which literally means *the word of hearing, the word which is heard* (1 Thessalonians 2:13; Hebrews 4:2). Certainly in the beginning it was in terms of speech and not of writing, in terms of persons and not of books that the Church thought—and it still remains true that the best epistle of all is a living epistle known and read of all men (2 Corinthians 3:2).

It may be that in the early Church the order of teachers has never been given its true importance. The teachers are mentioned in 1 Corinthians 12:28; Acts 13:1; Ephesians 4:11; Hebrews 5:12. The teachers must have been the men in every Christian community who knew the Christian story and who taught it to those who entered the Church long before there were any Christian books. The teachers must have been the living repositories of the Gospel story.

But as we have seen, the day came when a written gospel became a necessity. We know that the Gospels as we have them are not first attempts. We know, for instance, that before the Gospels emerged in their completed form there must have existed a kind of source book on the teaching of Jesus on which both Matthew and Luke freely drew. To that source book, which of course does not now exist, scholars give the symbol Q, which stands for the German word *quelle*—a source. We know also that it is highly probable that there was a book of *Testimonia*, *ie* a collection of Old Testament prophetic passages with their fulfilments in the life of Jesus. We know that there must have been many Gospels in circulation, for Luke tells us that many had set their hands to the task of setting out the Christian story, and Luke's implication is that none of these earlier Gospels was wholly satisfactory.

We know too that the Gospels of our New Testament must have had their rivals and competitors, for we have already noted that Jerome spoke of those 'who have attempted without the Spirit and the grace of God to draw up a story rather than to defend the truth of history'. Cyril of Jerusalem says: 'The four Gospels alone belong to the New Testament; the rest are *pseudepigrapha* [that is, written under assumed names and falsely attributed to great apostolic figures] and harmful' (Cyril, *Catecheses*

4.36). Just what the steps in the process were we do not know, but it is clear that it was not long before our four Gospels triumphed over all their rivals and became supreme. We may say that from the beginning our four Gospels had a ring of truth and the Spirit of God about them, which was obvious to every honest reader and seeker.

A Written Gospel

The first instance, when the word Gospel, *euaggelion*, comes to mean a written gospel come from very early in the second century. The *Didache*, the book known as the Teaching of the Twelve Apostles, introduces the Lord's Prayer with the words: 'Do not pray as the hypocrites, but as the Lord commanded in his Gospel' (*Didache* 8.2). Ignatius speaks of those who say that if they do not find a thing in the chapters in the Gospel, they do not believe (Ignatius, *Philadelphians* 8.2). Polycarp speaks of the Apostles who brought us the Gospel (Philippians 6.3).

When we trace the story, we find that the progress of the four Gospels is triumphant and apparently almost unopposed. Justin Martyr (AD 110-165) quotes copiously, although not accurately, but practically never from anything other than our Gospels. Theophilus of Antioch (*circa* AD 170) is the first to quote the New Testament as a definitely inspired work on a level with the prophets of the Old Testament. He quotes from John 1:14, 'The Word became flesh and dwelt among us', and says that it is the word of a Spirit-bearing man called John. Origen (AD 182-250) speaks of 'the four Gospels which alone are undisputed in the Church of God under heaven' (Eusebius, *The Ecclesiastical History* 6.25.3). And Athanasius in his Easter Letter in AD 367 mentions no other Gospel but our four. It may be said that our four Gospels held

D

undisputed sway long before AD 200. Very occasionally we come across quotations from, or references to, other Gospels, but as far back as we can go, our four Gospels are the fundamental documents of the Christian Church.

One final point emerges. Did the Church always intend to have four Gospels, or did it ever have the intention of reducing or unifying them into one? The existence of four different Gospels obviously presents difficulties. For instance, the genealogies of Jesus in Matthew and Luke are different: John places the cleansing of the Temple at the beginning of the ministry of Jesus, the other three Gospels at the end; the first three Gospels declare that Jesus was crucified *after* the Passover, and John says that he was crucified *before* the Passover; and there are undoubted differences in the Resurrection narratives in the different Gospels.

Did the Church ever have any intention of somehow making the four Gospels into one? There was in fact a deliberate attempt to do so. Sometime about AD 180 Tatian produced the *Diatessaron*—*dia* means *through* and *tessaron* means *four*—which was the first harmony of the four Gospels. For a time it was a very influential book, and it seemed possible that it might even supplant the four Gospels. But in the end it utterly failed to do so; it failed so completely that for many years it was completely lost.

In fact the swing away from any idea of one composite Gospel was so complete that we find Irenaeus (AD 125-200) insisting that the fourfold Gospel is in the very nature of things:

'As there are four quarters of the world in which we live, as there are four universal winds, and as the Church is scattered over all the earth, and the Gospel is the pillar and base of the Church and the breath of life, it is likely that it should have four pillars breathing immortality on every side and kindling afresh the life of men. Whence it is evident that the Word, the architect of all things, who sitteth upon the cherubim and holdeth all things together, having been made manifest unto men, gave to us the Gospel in a fourfold shape, but held together by one Spirit'

(Irenaeus, *Against Heresies* 3.11.8)

Later Jerome was to take the four corners and four rings by which the ark of the Covenant was carried as a symbol of the four Gospels (see the Prologue to the Four Gospels in the commentary of Matthew). The Church without hesitation retained the four Gospels and still without hesitation turned away from any attempt to turn them into one, in spite of the undoubted problems that the fourfold Gospel raised. Why should that have been? Well, it was due to the dominating importance of apostolic witness and apostolic testimony. No document which bore the name of Matthew or of John, no document which was thought to go back to Peter or to Paul could possibly be discarded. The Gospels were apostolic, and were, there-fore, the essential documents of the Christian faith.

We have still to reach the position when the Gospels are sacred and Holy Scripture, but already, midway through the second century, our four Gospels held a place of un-doubted and unquestioned authority within the Church.

Authoritative and Sacred

As we have seen, the Pauline Epistles and the Gospels came to be regarded as authoritative Christian books as groups, and along with them the Book of Acts gained full acceptance. The other books of the New Testament gained authority in a much more piecemeal way, just as the Old Testament Writings did; and we must postpone the story of their acceptance and entry into the Canon in order to look at a very important question and a very important development.

The question we are now bound to ask is—How did these books come to be regarded and set apart as *Scripture*? How and when did they cross the line between being books which were regarded as important and even authoritative, and books which were regarded as holy and sacred and inspired and the word of God? How, to put it in one word, did they become *canonical*? There is more than one answer to this question:

(1) Without question the books which are Scripture and which are truly the word of God have about them a self-evidencing quality. They carry their uniqueness on their face. To read them is to be conscious of being brought into the presence of God and truth and Jesus Christ in a unique way. They have always exercised, and still exercise, a quite unparalleled power upon the lives of men. In *The Bible in World Evangelism,* A M Chirgwin cites a whole series of stories to illustrate this unique power of Scripture. In Brazil there was a certain Signor Antonio of Minas. A friend urged him to consider the claims of Christ and again and again tried to make him accept a Bible. Finally he took the Bible—with the sole idea of taking it home to burn it. When he arrived home, the fire was out, but such was his determination to burn this book that he rekindled it. He opened the Bible so that it would burn more easily and he was just about to throw it into the fire. It opened at the Sermon on the Mount, and he glanced at the words. 'The words had in them something that held him. He read on, forgetful of time, through the hours of the night, and, just as the dawn was breaking, he stood up and declared, "I believe".'

A gangster in New York was released from prison after serving a sentence for robbery and violence. He was on his way to join his old associates to plan another exploit in crime. As he went along Fifth Avenue in New York, he picked a man's pocket. He slipped into Central Park to see what his haul consisted of, and he found himself in possession of a New Testament. Since he was too early for his appointment with his fellow-criminals, he sat down and idly began to read the book. 'Soon he was deep in the book, and he read to such effect that a few hours later he went to his comrades, and told them bluntly what he had been doing, and broke with them for good.' Here is the unique effect of the Bible. Its power is self-evidencing. When Coleridge was asked what he meant by the inspiration of the Bible, he said that he could give no other answer than to say: 'It finds me'.

In other words, it is the simple truth to say that the New Testament books became canonical because no one could stop them doing so. There were other books circulating; and there were even other books which in certain Churches enjoyed for a brief time a position in which they might possibly have entered the Canon. Many of these books we still possess; and we can say that to read them and then to read the New Testament is to enter into a different world.

(2) Certain books began to be read at the public worship of the Church. We have seen as early as Justin Martyr (AD 150) that what Justin called *The Memoirs of the Apostles,* which was the title by which he described the Gospels, were an essential part of the Christian service (Justin Martyr, *First Apology* 1.67). Clement of Rome wrote a letter to the Church at Corinth, and Eusebius tells us of a letter of Dionysius of Corinth, written about AD 175, in which Dionysius says that it was still the custom in his day to read Clement's letter at public worship (Eusebius, *The Ecclesiastical History* 4.23.10). And, as Harnack pertinently asked, if the letter of Clement was read, how much more would the much greater letters of

Paul be read in the Churches to which they were sent, and in other Churches which knew of them? Books which were read at the worship of the Church had a special position, and had at least begun on the road that lead to their full entry into the Canon of Scripture.

Discarding the Old Testament

(3) But something happened which forced the hand of the Church. About AD 140 there came to the Church in Rome a man called Marcion. Marcion was a wealthy and much-travelled ship-owner from Sinope, and he was generous with his money to the Church at Rome. Marcion was a Gnostic, and a knowledge of the broad principles of Gnosticism is necessary to understand Marcion's position and the Church's reaction to him.

The Gnostics believed that they possessed a special and an inner knowledge which had come to them direct from the secret teaching of the Apostles, or even from the secret teaching of Jesus himself. It was an essential principle of the Gnostics that the whole universe was founded on a dualism. They believed that spirit and matter were both eternal. God is pure spirit, and altogether good. Matter is essentially flawed and evil. Since matter is eternal, the world was not created out of nothing; it was created out of this essentially flawed matter. God being altogether good could never directly touch or handle this flawed matter. So God put out a series of emanations called *aeons*. As each aeon was further from God, so each was more and more ignorant of God. As the aeons proceeded down this scale, they became not only ignorant of God, but actually hostile to God. At last in the series there emerged an aeon so distant from God that he could touch and handle evil matter and thus create the world. This creating aeon was called the *Demiurge*. From this it can be seen that the Gnostics believed that the God of creation is quite different from and quite hostile to the true God. It was in this way that they explained the sin and sorrow and suffering and evil of the world.

This kind of belief had many serious consequences. It had serious consequences on their beliefs about Jesus. If matter is evil, then Jesus could never have had a real body, and therefore he was nothing other than a kind of spiritual phantom with only the appearance of a body. If the body is evil, one of two courses follows. Either the body must be denied and starved and kept down in a rigid asceticism, or the body does not matter, and therefore its instincts may be sated and glutted in a wild antinomianism.

But in the case of Marcion and in regard to the Canon of the New Testament, Gnosticism had very definite consequences. The Gnostics identified the ignorant, hostile God of creation with the God of the Old Testament, who, they said, was a quite different God from the God of the New Testament whom Jesus had revealed. Sometimes this made them, as it were, turn the Old Testament upside down. If the God of the Old Testament is an ignorant and inferior God, hostile to the true God, then the people he punished are the good people, and the people he blessed are the bad people. So there were some Gnostics who believed Cain and Korah and Baalam to be the heroes of the Old Testament, and who actually worshipped the serpent as the representative of the true God. In particular most kinds of Gnosticism obviously demanded the complete and total abandonment of the Old Testament and all those that had to do with the Old Testament as the work and the words of the evil God.

In view of this attitude to the Old Testament, Marcion very naturally produced his own Canon of Scripture. In it the Old Testament was completely discarded. The Old Testament had held three parts—the Law, the Prophets, and the Writings. In place of the Law Marcion put the *Gospel*. He discarded Matthew, Mark and John as being far too much tinged with Judaism, and in place of them substituted an expurgated version of Luke, from which every Old Testament reference had been removed. In place of the Prophets he substituted the *Apostle*, in which he included ten letters of Paul, whom he regarded as the great enemy of the old Law and the great exponent of the new gospel. The ten letters were Galatians, 1 and 2 Corinthians, Romans, 1 and 2 Thessalonians, Laodiceans (arguing from Colossians 4:16, he regarded Ephesians as having been written to Laodicea), Colossians, Philippians, and Philemon. For the Writings he substituted a book of his own called the *Antitheses* in which he compiled a list of Old Testament passages with the New Testament contradictions of them.

This presented the Church with a real problem. Here was a heretic who had compiled a Canon of Scripture for himself while the Church still officially had none. The greatest problem of all was the position of Paul. Marcion worshipped Paul barely this side of idolatry. As he saw it, Paul was the great enemy of the Law, and the great bringer of the Gospel. For Marcion, Paul was the supreme figure in the Church. He held that in heaven Paul sits at the right hand of Christ, who sits at the right hand of God. He held that Paul was the promised *Paraclete*, the Comforter whom Jesus had promised to his followers. Christ, he said, had descended from heaven twice, once to suffer and die, and once to call Paul and reveal to him the true significance of Christ's death. As Tertullian ironically put it, Paul had become the apostle of the heretics. Of course, Marcion had to misinterpret Paul to make Paul fit his beliefs, but the impression was that Paul had been annexed and appropriated by the heretics. So then Marcion, as Tertullian stated, 'criticized the Scriptures with a penknife,' cutting off the parts which did not suit him, and forming his own Canon. The Church *had* to act.

The Church's Decision

The Church *had* to act: the Church had to say which books it did regard as Holy Scripture. And what was to happen to Paul? Was he to be abandoned to the heretics, or was he to be legitimized? It could be argued that Paul was no apostle because he was not one of the original twelve; it could be argued that his letters contained statements which could be used as a basis for heresy; and it was true that the heretics had well-nigh made him their patron saint. Paul's fate was swinging in the balance.

But two things rescued Paul. First, his letters were read in all the Churches, and were very effective in the spread and defence of the Gospel. Second, there was the Book of Acts. In it Paul was set forth in all the glory of his apostleship, and it was proved in it that Christ had called him and that the Twelve had accepted him.

That is why Acts comes where it does in the order of the New Testament books. Logically Acts should come after Luke, of which it is the second volume, but in point of fact it comes between the Gospels and the letters of Paul, because it is the bridge between them, and it is the document which guarantees that the letters which follow are the letters of an Apostle, and of the greatest of the Apostles. Acts provides Paul's title to apostolicity, and, therefore, immediately precedes his letters.

So the Church finally legitimized Paul. It further sought out such additional apostolic materials as it possessed, and it finally arrived at a list. That list, it is fairly certain, is embodied in a document called the *Muratorian Canon*, which takes its name from its discoverer L A Muratori, who first published it in 1740. The *Muratorian Canon* is damaged at the beginning, and actually begins with Luke, but its list of books is as follows—Matthew, Mark, Luke, John, Acts, 1 and 2 Corinthians, Ephesians, Philippians, Colossians, Galatians, 1 and 2 Thessalonians, Romans, Philemon, Titus, 1 and 2 Timothy, Jude, 1 and 2 John, the Apocalypse of John (that is, the Revelation), the Apocalypse of Peter. To this list is added The Wisdom of Solomon.

Here, then, is the first list of the New Testament Canon. The date of the Muratorian Canon is about AD 170, and these are the books which at that time the Church accepted as sacred Scripture. The only startling omission is the omission of 1 Peter, and although it is absent from this list, it may be regarded as certain that the Church even then did accept it.

Already the Canon is taking shape. The omitted books —James, 2 Peter, 3 John, Hebrews—are precisely the books which took longest and had the hardest struggle to enter the Canon, and to their history we shall later return. The New Testament is well on the way to being finalized —and the strange thing is that the stimulus to this first step was the work and influence of Marcion the heretic, and the enemy of true Christianity.

Closing of the Books

(4) The process of canonization was, therefore, begun by a heretic, and it is a curious fact that it was also completed by a heretic, or at least completed in principle. How did it come about that the Canon of the New Testament was closed? Christianity has always been a religion of the Spirit: according to the Fourth Gospel, Jesus had promised to his people ever greater and greater revelations and insights into the truth (John 16:12). How then did there ever come a time when the Church declared that all the

inspired books that could be written had been written, and that nothing more could ever be added to the written word of God? How did it come about that, as Tertullian bitterly said, 'the Holy Spirit was chased into a book'?

In the second half of the second century a change was coming over the Church. The days of enthusiasm were passing and the days of ecclesiasticism were arriving. No more was the Church a place in which the spirit of prophecy was a commonplace. People were flooding into the Church. No more was there the sharp distinction between Church and world. The Church was becoming secularized; it was coming to terms with heathen thought and culture and philosophy. The Christian ethic was tending to become less lofty, and the Christian demand less absolute.

Into this situation, between AD 156 and 172, there came a man called Montanus. He had once been a priest of Cybele, he had been converted to Christianity; and he emerged in Asia Minor, bearing a demand for a higher standard and a greater discipline and sharper separation of the Church from the world. Had he halted there, he could have a lot of good; when Montanism did settle down and purge itself of its extravagances, in the days when Tertullian became a Montanist in AD 202, that was the emphasis of Montanist teaching. But Montanus himself went much further. He and his two prophetesses, Prisca and Maximilla, went about prophesying in the name of the Spirit, foretelling the speedy second coming of Christ. More, Montanus claimed to be the promised *Paraclete*, come with a new vision and a new message for the Church. He was convinced that he and his prophetesses were the God-given instruments of revelation, the lyres across which the Spirit swept to draw new music: a dangerous tendency.

'When Montanus said, "I am the Father and the Son and the Paraclete", he had manifestly crossed the line which separates fervour from extravagance. When one prophetess declared that Christ, in the form of a woman, slept with her, she was on the verge of something more repulsive.'

(W D Niven, *The Conflicts of the Early Church*)

Clearly this was a situation in which the Church had to act. Montanus as a herald of a new spiritual vitality and a new challenge to holiness was one thing; Montanus as the claimant to divine revelation was quite another. It was in the face of this new situation that the Church decided that Scripture was closed, that the book of the new covenant was signed and sealed, that the basic Christian documents were written. The result of Montanism was the decision in principle that the Canon of Scripture was completed and closed.

So, then, by the end of the second century the Church had reached a position in which the Canon of the New Testament was well on the way to being defined, and in which, in principle, it was agreed that the production of sacred Scripture had come to an end.

The Final Completion

We must now move on to the final step in the completion of the Canon of the New Testament. In this we are fortunate enough to have excellent evidence, for two of the greatest scholars of the early Church made deliberate investigations into the status of the various New Testament books in their day, and the results of these investigations have come down to us.

Origen (AD 182-251), who was the greatest scholar the early Church ever had, investigated the matter, and his conclusions are passed down to us by Eusebius (*The Ecclesiastical History* 6.25.7-14). The following books he regards as beyond question part of the New Testament —the four Gospels, the letters of Paul, including Hebrews, 1 Peter, 1 John, the Apocalypse. He says that Peter may have left a second letter, 'but this is doubtful'. Of 2 and 3 John he says that 'not all consider them genuine'. Acts he does not mention in his catalogue, but he certainly accepted it. James and Jude he does not list at all. He thinks that Hebrews has some connection with Paul, and he never doubts the excellence of its thought and its right to a place in the New Testament. He may well have known the opinion of Clement of Alexandria that Paul wrote it in Hebrew and that Luke translated it into Greek; he hands down the opinion of some that Clement of Rome wrote it. But his own verdict is: 'Who wrote the letter, God alone knows'.

Eusebius of Caesarea (AD 270-340) made a similar investigation. He divided the books into three classes —the *homologoumena*, which are accepted by everyone; the *antilegomena*, which are disputed; and the *notha*—the word means bastard—which are spurious and to be definitely rejected (*The Ecclesiastical History* 3.25). The *universally accepted* books are the Four Gospels, Acts, the letters of Paul including Hebrews, 1 John, and 1 Peter. The Revelation is in an intermediate position. Eusebius lists it with the accepted books, with the comment, 'If it really seems proper', and notes that some reject it. The *disputed books* are 'the so-called' letter of James, Jude, 2 Peter, 'those that are called 2 and 3 John, whether they belong to the evangelist or another person of the same name'. Elsewhere he is more definite about 2 Peter (*The Ecclesiastical History* 3.3), for he says: 'We have learned that Peter's extant second letter does not belong to the Canon; yet, as it has appeared profitable to many, it has been used with the other Scriptures'. He is also elsewhere (*The Ecclesiastical History* 2.23.25) more definite about

James. In his notice on the life of James he says: 'James is said to be the author of the first of the so-called Catholic Epistles; but it is to be observed that it is regarded as spurious, at least not many of the ancients have mentioned it'; and he goes on to include Jude under the same verdict.

So then, by AD 300 it is quite certain that the New Testament contained the following indisputable books —the four Gospels, Acts, fourteen letters of Paul including Hebrews, 1 Peter, 1 John, and the Revelation with just a tinge of doubt. Still on the fringe of the New Testament were James, 2 Peter, 2 and 3 John, Jude, although Jude was included as early as the Muratorian Canon. We must be quite clear about these books against which there was a question mark. Their usefulness for life and doctrine is not in question; they were freely used and freely quoted; there is no question of their rejection. Eusebius supplies a list of books which were definitely rejected—the Shepherd of Hermas, the Apocalypse of Peter, the Letter of Barnabas, the so-called Teaching of the Apostles. Although Eusebius and Origen list these books as disputed, they never suggest discarding them.

What, then, was the real trouble about these books? The real trouble was that the test of the Church for any book, as we have seen, was apostolicity, and no one was quite sure who had written these books. No one, for instance, questioned the value of Hebrews, but the trouble was that no one knew who had written it, although Tertullian states for a fact that it is the work of Barnabas (*Concerning Modesty* 20). That is why in the end Hebrews was attributed to Paul (although it was clear enough that Paul did not write it), why James was attributed to the brother of our Lord, Jude to another of Jesus' brothers, 2 Peter to Peter, 2 and 3 John to John. These were of a value which no one disputed, and the only way to bring them fully into the Canon of Scripture was to shelter them under the wing of an Apostle. And it is certainly true that, even if they are not the work of the Apostles whose name they came to bear, they are certainly apostolic.

We have very nearly come to the full-grown New Testament. There are still two steps. Cyril of Jerusalem (AD 315-386), in his lectures to those being prepared for membership of the Church, lists the books of the New Testament—the Four Gospels, the Acts of the Twelve Apostles, the seven Catholic Epistles, one of James, two of Peter, three of John, one of Jude, and lastly, 'as the seal of all', the fourteen letters of Paul (*Catechetical Lectures* 4.36). Here the list is complete save only for the Revelation.

And so we come to the final step. In his Easter Letter of AD 367, Athanasius finally lists the full New Testament. His letter is such a landmark that the relevant passage of it must be quoted in full:

'There must be no hesitation to state again the books of the New Testament, for they are these: Four Gospels, according to Matthew, according to Mark, according to Luke, and according to John. Further, after these also, the Acts of the Apostles, and the seven so-called Catholic Epistles of the Apostles, as follows: one of James, but two of Peter, then three of John, and after these one of Jude. In addition to these there are fourteen Epistles of the Apostle Paul put down in the following order: the first to the Romans, then two to the Corinthians, and after these the Epistles to the Galatians and then to the Ephesians: further, the Epistles to the Philippians and to the Colossians and two to the Thessalonians, and the Epistle to the Hebrews. And next two letters to Timothy, but one to Titus, and the last one to Philemon. Moreover also, the Apocalypse of John.'

There stands our New Testament, and, apart from the fact that the Catholic Epistles are placed after Acts, as they are in all early manuscripts, not only the list but the order of the books is the order we possess today. The Canon of the New Testament is complete.

Part III

The Final Test

THERE IS ONE last question to ask—What is it that makes a book sacred and holy Scripture? What is it that makes a book part of the word of God? What is it that entitles a book to a place among the canonical books of the Church? More than one answer has been, and still is, given to that question.

Authority of the Books

(1) The answer of the Roman Catholic Church is clear and unequivocal. A book becomes a canonical book by the tradition, the authority and the decision of the Church. In 1546 the Council of Trent listed the books which for the Roman Catholic Church form the Old and the New Testaments, and then said that if any man did not accept the list whole and entire, *each book* whole and entire, he was anathema. In the Roman Catholic Church there is nothing more to be said; these books are canonical, and there can be no demur and no dispute.

(2) For the Reformers the case was different. To base anything on the tradition and the authority of the Church was precisely and exactly what they could not do. It has often been said that the Protestant Church did no more than substitute an infallible book for an infallible Church; but it must be remembered that the Reformers were well aware of the critical history of the books of the New Testament, and were fully prepared to give that critical history its full place in the evaluation of a book. When

Oecolampadius the Swiss reformer was consulted by the Waldensians about the constitution of the Canon of the New Testament, he named the twenty-seven of them, but at the same time he pointed out that six of them—he did not include Hebrews—were *antilegomena*, disputed books, and that they held inferior rank within the New Testament. 'The Apocalypse together with the letters of James and Jude and the second letter of Peter and the two letters of John we do not compare with the rest of the books.' The Reformers were not in the least fundamentalists, if that word be taken to describe those who insist that every word of Scripture is equally inspired, equally sacred, and equally infallible.

(3) Curiously enough, the one reformer who wrote on the Canon in particular took up a position which is very closely connected with the Roman Catholic position. That reformer was Andreas Bodenstein of Karlstadt. He applied one test—the test of attestation. The earlier and the greater the attestation to any book, the higher the rank he gave that book within the Canon. On this basis he divided all the biblical books into three classes:

The first class contained the five books of Moses and the four Gospels, which are in a class by themselves, and which are 'the most brilliant lamps of divine truth' (*totius veritatis divinae clarissima lumina*).

The second class contained the Prophets—Joshua, Judges, Ruth, Samuel, Kings, Isaiah, Jeremiah with Lamentations, Ezekiel and the Twelve, together with the fifteen undoubted New Testament letters—thirteen of Paul, one of Peter, and one of John.

The third class contained the Writings of the Old Testament, and the seven disputed books of the New Testament —he included Hebrews—which occupy the very lowest rank in the Canon. If we apply this test, then the Revelation and Hebrews rank below James, Jude and John, because they were later in gaining a settled and secure and final place in the Canon. The one test is, how early did a book gain admission to the Canon, and how fully is it attested? The odd fact about this is that to all intents and purposes it settles canonicity by the tradition of the Church, which is precisely what the Roman Catholic Church does.

(4) There is the test of Calvin. Calvin's test may be defined as the witness of the Holy Spirit within a man, answering to the witness of the Holy Spirit within the book. Calvin was no obscurantist. He is quite certain that Hebrews is not the work of Paul, yet he has no hesitation in using Hebrews magnificently for commenting on, for preaching on, and for doctrine. He declares that it is by no means clear who wrote James, and that the author may well not have been the Apostle, but he gladly and willingly accepts the book as Scripture. In regard to 2 Peter, Calvin is critically ready to agree that it is not the work of Peter, but that position does not for him in the least detract from the religious value of the letter. He does not comment at all on the Revelation, but that does not mean that he gave it an inferior place. For Calvin the test of canonicity is certainly not ecclesiastical tradition; it is equally not apostolic authorship; it is in the last analysis 'religious intuition'. For Calvin the ultimate test of canonicity was nothing other than the witness of the Spirit.

Does the Book Speak of Christ?

(5) Of all the Reformers, Luther had the best defined and in many ways the most logical position. Luther's one test was—Does a book speak of Christ? It is that test which enables Luther to treat Scripture with an amazing freedom. In the concluding paragraph of his Preface to the New Testament, he writes:

'In sum: the Gospel and the First Epistle of John, St Paul's Epistles, especially those to the Romans, Galatians, and Ephesians, and St Peter's First Epistle are the books which show Christ to you. They teach everything you need to know for your salvation, even if you were never to see or hear any other book, or hear any other teaching. In comparison with these the Epistle of James is an Epistle full of straw, because it contains nothing evangelical.'

Here is the touchstone, and then there comes the startling passage: 'That which does not teach Christ is not apostolic, though Peter or Paul should have said it; on the contrary, that which does preach Christ is apostolic, even if it should come from Judas, Annas, Herod, or Pilate.'

It is for this reason that Luther felt able to make an actual division in his New Testament as it was printed. There were four books to which Luther gave an inferior place. James derives justification from works; it contradicts Paul; it has nothing to say about the life, death, resurrection or Spirit of Jesus. Hebrews in three places (chapters 6,10,12) refuses repentance to sinners after baptism, contrary to all the Gospels and all Paul's Epistles. Jude is useless because it has nothing fundamental to the Christian faith, and is only an extract from 2 Peter. In the Apocalypse there are unintelligible and unbiblical images and visions, and the author had the audacity to add promises and threats about obeying and disobeying his words, when no one knows what his words mean. So, then, on the title page of his New Testament, Luther printed these four books in a group by themselves with a space between them and the other twenty-three. Further, he numbered the other twenty-three but left these unnumbered. He quite definitely relegated them to a lesser position. He can admire them; he can admire the austerity of James and eulogize the doctrine of Christ as High Priest in Hebrews, but these books do not manifest Christ, and, therefore, they were not for Luther. There was no point in quoting proof texts to Luther. 'If,' he said, 'in the debates in which exegesis brings no decisive victories, our adversaries press the letter against Christ, we shall insist on Christ against the letter.'

He is equally severe on the Old Testament. Of Ecclesiastes, he said: 'This book ought to be more complete; it wants many things; it has neither boots nor spurs, and rides in simple sandals as I used to do when I was still in the convent. Solomon is not its author'. The books of Kings and Chronicles are only the calendars of the Jews, containing the list of their kings and their kind of government. 'As for the second book of Maccabees and that of Esther,' he writes, 'I dislike them so much that I wish they did not exist; for they are too Jewish and have many bad pagan elements.'

One thing is to be remembered. Luther granted to others the freedom which he demanded of himself. He did not wish to impose his own views on anyone. In the Preface to James he writes: 'I cannot place it among the right canonical works, but I do not wish thereby to prevent anyone from so placing it and extolling it as seems good to him'. In the Preface to Revelation he writes: 'In this book I leave it to every man to make out his own meaning; I wish no one to be bound to my views or opinion . . . Let every man hold what his spirit gives him'. Of Hebrews he says that it does not lay the foundation of the faith, but nevertheless the writer does build gold, silver, precious stones (1 Corinthians 3:12), even if there is wood, straw, and hay intermingled. 'We should receive such fine doctrine with all honour.' Luther gave to others the rights he claimed himself.

Faith is a Living Saviour

In the last analysis Luther is right. The great test of any book of Scripture is—In it do we find Jesus Christ? For in the last analysis it is not upon any book that our faith is built, but on a living Saviour.

The story of the making of the Bible is a story which enables us to see the supreme value of the books of the Bible as nothing else can or does. It enables us to see that these books did not become Scripture by the decision of any Church or any man; they became Scripture because out of them men and women found comfort in times of their own sorrow, hope in their despair, strength in their weakness, power in their temptation, light in their darkness, faith in their uncertainty, and in their sin a Saviour. That is why the Bible is *the word* of God.

When the Church did make its canonical lists, it was not choosing and selecting these books; it was only affirming and attesting that these already were the books on which men had stayed their hearts and fed their souls. And that is why there never can be a time when the Church or the Christian can do without this Bible which has always been the word of God to his people, and the place where men find Jesus Christ.

Bibliography

PUBLISHER'S NOTE

The following list includes only the books used in the preparation of this study. Titles from the author's original bibliography which are still available at the time of this revision are denoted with an asterisk.

Bewer, J A: *The Literature of the Old Testament*, New York 1947.

Buhl, F: *Canon and Text of the Old Testament*, translated by J Macpherson, Edinburgh 1892.

Charteris, A H: *Canonicity: early Testimonies to the Canonical Books of the New Testament*, Edinburgh 1880.

Cornhill, C: *Introduction to the Canonical Books of the Old Testament*, translated by G H Box, London 1907.

*Driver, S R: *Introduction to the Literature of the Old Testament*, T & T Clark, Edinburgh (ninth edition dated 1913 used by Author).

Filson, Floyd V: *Which Book belong in the Bible? A Study of The Canon*, Philadelphia 1957.

Goodspeed, Edgar Johnson: *An Introduction to the New Testament*, Chicago 1937.

Goodspeed, Edgar Johnson: *The Formation of the New Testament*, Chicago 1926.

Grant, F C: *The Gospels, their Origin and Growth*, 1957.

Gregory, C R: *Canon and Text of the New Testament*, Edinburgh 1907.

Harnack, Adolf von: *Bible Reading in the Early Church,*
    translated by J R Wilkinson, London 1912.

Harnack, Adolf von: *The Origin of the New Testament,*
    translated by J R Wilkinson, London 1925.

Knox, J: *Philemon among the Letters of Paul* 1959.

McNeile, A H: *An Introduction to the Study of the New
    Testament,* revised by C S C Williams, Oxford 1952.

Mitton, C Leslie: *The Formation of the Pauline Corpus of
    Letters,* London 1955.

*Moffatt, James: *An Introduction to the Literature of the
    New Testament,* International Theology Library, T & T
    Clark, Edinburgh (third edition dated 1918 used by
    Author).

Moore, G F: *Judaism in the first Centuries of the Christian
    Era,* three volumes, Harvard and Cambridge 1932.

Moore, G F:*The Literature of the Old Testament,* revised
    by L H Brockington, Oxford 1948.

Niven, W D: *Conflicts of the Early Church,* London 1930

Pfeiffer, Robert Henry: *Introduction to the Old Testament,*
    New York 1941

* Pfeiffer, Robert Henry: *History of New Testament Times,
    with an Introduction to the Apocrypha,* Greenwood
    Press, London (1949 US edition used by Author).

Redlich, E Basil: *The Student's Introduction to the Synoptic
    Gospels,* London 1936.

Redlich, E Basil: *Form Criticism, its Value and Limitations,*
    London 1939.

Reuss, E: *History of the Canon of the Holy Scriptures,*
    translated by D Hunter, Edinburgh 1891.

Rowley, H: *The Growth of the Old Testament,* 1949.

Ryle, H: *The Canon of the Old Testament,* Cambridge 1892.

Smith, W R: *The Old Testament in the Jewish Church,*
    second edition, Edinburgh 1892.

Souter, A: *The Text and Canon of the New Testament,*
    revised by C S C Williams, London 1954.

Theron, D J: *The Evidence of Tradition*, London 1959.
Westcott, B F: *General Survey of the History of the Canon of the New Testament*, seventh edition, London 1896.
Wildeboar, G: *The Origin of the Canon of the Old Testament*, translated by B W Bacon, London 1895.

Notes

Notes

Notes

Notes

Notes

Notes